# THE
# EMERGENCE
## OF A
# WORLD
# CHRISTIAN COMMUNITY

*The Rockwell Lectures on Religion*
*at the Rice Institute, Houston, Texas*

## KENNETH SCOTT LATOURETTE

D. WILLIS JAMES PROFESSOR OF MISSIONS AND ORIENTAL HISTORY
IN YALE UNIVERSITY

PUBLISHED FOR THE RICE INSTITUTE

BY

YALE UNIVERSITY PRESS · NEW HAVEN

LONDON · GEOFFREY CUMBERLEGE · OXFORD UNIVERSITY PRESS

1949

# PREFACE

ONE of the most striking facts of our time is the global extension of Christianity and the fashion in which the Christians of the world are beginning to come together. Never before has it or any other religion been as widely extended geographically or as deeply rooted among so many peoples as has Christianity in the present century. The chief strength of Christianity is still in the Occident, but the growth among non-Occidental peoples has been phenomenal. Moreover, Christians are drawing together as never before. Until the new trend the record of Christianity has been one of multiplying divisions. Attempts at bringing into one visible fellowship all those who profess and call themselves Christians had been progressively less successful. Now the tide has turned. Not only is Christianity becoming world wide in its extent: this world-wide Christianity is being knit into a community. Organizationally this growing Christian unity is taking many and quite new forms. It is without precedent. The process is far from complete. It seems only to have begun. Certainly it is proceeding at an accelerated pace.

The emergence of a world Christian community is especially significant because of the age in which it is occurring. Mechanical inventions are making imperative the cooperation of all mankind. Improved methods of transportation and communication have brought all men physically together in a rapidly shrinking world. The very closeness of that association has accentuated friction between races and nations. Science has placed at his disposal weapons of offense and defense which man can turn to the destruction of his civilization and himself. The nations are slowly and painfully learning to work together, but it is an open question whether they will do so in time to avoid another series of armed conflicts which will send man hurtling into an abyss worse than barbarism. A spiritual and moral tie is desperately needed which will hasten wholesome cooperation and assure its success. The most hopeful prospect of such a tie is the growing world Christian fellowship.

The purpose of this little book is to describe the emerging world-wide Christian community. First there will be given a brief summary of the historical background to set the present in perspective and thus better to see its significance and to judge the direction which the future may be expected to take. Then will come a description of the present situation, with its weakness and achievements. Finally, as is fitting, there will be a statement of the unsolved problems and the prospect for their solution.

The subject, fortunately, is not new. On it much has been written and will be written. Because the movement is making such rapid headway no one can now hope to say the final word. Yet there is room for a brief summary and for the statement in clear and simple form of essential features of the historical background and the direction which must be taken if the movement is not to miscarry. Indeed, some of these features are in danger of being ignored.

The author deems himself fortunate to be given an opportunity by the Rockwell Lectures at the Rice Institute to attempt such a summary and to speak his mind on some of the crucial issues. The complete freedom afforded and, indeed, encouraged by the lectureship has made possible a frank and untrammeled expression of deeply held convictions. For the opportunity and the gracious hospitality of the officers and faculty of the Rice Institute and for the patient courtesy of his audiences the author is profoundly grateful.

# CONTENTS

# THE EMERGENCE OF A
# WORLD CHRISTIAN COMMUNITY

## I

### *The Historical Background*

BY ITS very genius Christianity aspires to bring all mankind into its fold and to knit all Christians into one united community of good will. The familiar "Great Commission," with its command to make disciples of all the nations, baptizing them, and teaching them to observe all that Jesus had commanded the inner circle of his immediate followers, is so breath-taking that many have questioned whether it is an authentic word of Jesus. It en tails the winning of all men to become conscious and deliberate adherents of Christ, the incorporation of them, by baptism, into the company of his followers, and such persuasive and compelling instruction that they all will eventually conform to the apparently impossible ideals set forth in the Sermon on the Mount, until they are perfect as God Himself is perfect.

Were the Great Commission an isolated and unique saying, we might agree with those who regard it as an addition by the second or third generation of Christians—although even then we would have to account for its formulation by those who were only slightly removed in time from Jesus and believed the saying to be in full conformity with his spirit. But in one form or another this vision is implicit or explicit in passage after passage in the Gospels. The familiar petition, which even the most skeptical acknowledge to be the words of Jesus, "thy kingdom come, thy will be done on earth as it is in heaven," cannot be fully answered unless the Great Commission is accomplished. "God sent not his son into the world to condemn the world, but that the world should be saved through him," clearly states the purpose of God to be to bring all men into transforming belief in His Son. The deeply moving prayer: "Neither for these only [i.e., the immediate disciples] do I pray, but for them also that believe on me through their word; that they may all be one; even as thou, Father, art in me, and I in thee, that they also may be one in us; that the world may believe that thou didst send me," has in it the profound desire that the entire world shall believe and that all men, believing, shall constitute an unbroken fellowship. The world is to be persuaded by the evidence of the power of love to make over self-seeking, quarrelsome men, and to create of them a single company of worship, trust, and service. Then, won to belief, the entire world is to be incorporated into that "blessed company."

The fulfillment of this dream has been so long delayed that it has seemed an impossibility. It is a goal which appears to taunt man. The best in man's nature responds with wistful yearning only to find itself frustrated by man's sin until it cries, despairing, "Oh, wretched man that I am, who shall deliver me from the body of this death?"

At the very beginning the outlook for the fulfillment appeared so slight that the dream seemed fantastic. Christ declared that in him God was inaugurating a new order of society, the Kingdom of Heaven, in which His will would be perfectly done and which would not be limited to time but would extend beyond history into eternity. Yet the cross appeared the brutal denial of that dream through the humiliating and pitiful death of the dreamer. Religious bigotry and blindness, callous political expediency, the self-interest of particular groups and classes, and mass hysteria seemed to have triumphed. The little band of followers, quite naturally not comprehending the vision or the only way, the cross, by which it could be made actual, was completely disheartened.

Even after the resurrection had transformed the disciples into convinced missionaries of their risen Lord, the prospect for their faith was still far from bright. To the worldling the disciples appeared to be only a minor Jewish sect, one of the most insignificant of the many faiths which were competing for the allegiance of the Roman Empire. When the unbelievable had happened and the overwhelming majority of the Roman Empire had become professedly Christian, only a minority of mankind had been won. The great mass of civilized mankind in Asia—in Persia, India, and China—had scarcely been affected, and primitive mankind, in possession of most of the five continents, had only here and there been touched. The very winning of the Roman Empire tended to identify Christianity with the Occident and so to preclude it from achieving universality: Christianity's first major geographic victory carried with it a handicap.

Until almost our own day, Christianity has been confined chiefly to one cultural stream, that of the Occident. To be sure, Christian minorities have from time to time been widely spread among peoples of other cultures. From the seventh to the fourteenth centuries groups of Nestorians were to be found intermittently from Mesopotamia to the China Sea and from central Asia to South India. In western Asia churches such as those of the Armenians, the Jacobites, and the Copts flourished outside the main currents of the Occident. The Roman Catholic missions of the sixteenth, seventeenth, and eighteenth centuries won to the faith millions of the Indians of the Americas and gave rise to small Christian communities along the shores of Africa, in the south and east of Asia, and in Japan. From the seventh century to the present Christianity has been more widely distributed and more nearly universal in geographic spread than has any other religion. Yet the Nestorians have all but disappeared, the Armenian (or Gregorian) Church has always been confined to one people and in the present century has suffered severe blows, and the Jacobite and Coptic churches have long been dwindling. Such remnants of these churches as survive are on the defensive, minorities encysted in a predominantly Moslem environment, or, in South India, in the prevailing Hinduism. In the Americas the Indian Roman Catholics have been dependent upon European leadership, have shown no significant inclination to propagate their faith among non-Christians, even on their own frontiers, and in quality of Christian living are distinctly inferior, a liability rather than an asset to their church. With rare exceptions, until the present century the Roman Catholic communities in Asia and Africa drew their bishops and most of their clergy from Europe and were, in effect, ecclesiastical colonies of a church which by its close association with Rome was overwhelmingly Occidental.

In addition to being Occidental rather than universal, Christianity has appeared hopelessly divided. Instead of being one, a single fellowship united in love and loyalty to a common Lord, Christians have quarreled bitterly, often over differing convictions about the most sacred mysteries of their faith. They have divided on such central issues as the nature of Jesus and his relation to God. Baptism, closely connected with the new birth into the life which Christ came to make possible for men, has been a bone of contention. Christians have found themselves unable to come together around the table which their Lord made forever sacred on the night before his crucifixion. Indeed, that table has become a symbol of division rather than of union.

Before the past century, divisions among Christians not

only multiplied: every major attempt at unity led to fresh schisms. Never have all those who have professed themselves to be followers of Christ been one. From the first generation of Christians, divisions have existed. Every reader of the New Testament is familiar with the sharp controversy between the kind of Christianity of which Paul was the champion and that which insisted upon full conformity with the Jewish ritual law. The latter, a waning remnant, persisted, as the Ebionites, for several generations. The New Testament also hints at other varieties of Christianity: we know of them through the sharp condemnations of their views which are contained in some of its pages. In the early centuries the Gnostics flourished and their opponents were excoriating in their denunciations. The Gnostics themselves were not united but displayed many variations. For generations the Marcionites, who had their origin in the second century, with their headquarters in Rome, offered serious competition to those who regarded themselves as orthodox.

In the third century what called itself the Catholic Church included in its membership the majority of the Christians of the Roman Empire. Probably it embraced within its structure a larger proportion of professed Christians than has any other one church before or since. In this achievement it was assisted by the unity of the political structure within which it arose. It had taken form within the Roman Empire and did not extend far beyond the boundaries of that realm. To be sure, until the fourth century the Roman Government was hostile, but the political, economic, and cultural unity which was furthered by Rome facilitated the creation of a united church within its borders. To this day the largest of the Christian churches bears the name of Rome, has its capital in that city, and in its structure and temper reflects to no small degree the organization and the genius of the Roman Empire.

The Roman Catholic way of achieving the unity which is of the essence of the Christian dream has proved futile. Beginning with the fourth century rifts appeared which issued in fresh and permanent divisions. In time Arians, Nestorians, Monophysites, Donatists, and others were expelled from the Catholic Church. As the centuries passed an increasing proportion of Christians dissented from it. Although the Roman Catholic Church is strong and vigorous and is still expanding, the expansion is predominantly by an excess of births over deaths and by conversion from non-Christian communities. Only a relatively few are coming from other Christian bodies. Accessions from Protestantism and from the older Eastern churches, even when the Uniate bodies are included, are numerically small minorities and although sometimes spectacular are of no great significance. Even now the Roman Catholic Church is losing more to Protestant churches than it is gaining from them and from all Christian bodies. The progress of Protestantism among nominally Roman Catholic populations in Latin America and the Philippines is striking. Many of the Roman Catholic clergy and laity display great devotion and undeniable beauty of Christian living. The prayers of thousands for the unity of all Christians through what they hold to be the divinely appointed way, namely, the Roman Catholic Church, are undoubtedly sincere. Yet the fact remains that increasingly across the centuries the Roman Catholic road to Christian unity has been a blind alley.

During the Middle Ages the Roman Catholic Church held in one fold the large majority of the Christians of western Europe, but the Greek East drifted away from it. The Roman and Orthodox churches became separate, out of communion with each other. In other words, when the political tie of the Roman Empire was dissolved, the church which inherited the Roman name and tradition proved unable to hold together across the barriers of nationality and language the Christians in the communities which were once comprised in that empire.

The Roman Catholic Church by no means entirely failed. It kept within its fellowship the Greek-speaking peoples of southern Italy, but the tie was as much geographic as religious. In western Europe, in the political disorder which followed the disintegration of the Roman Empire the Roman Catholic Church won the non-Christian barbarians to the faith and knit them together in a common culture of which it was in large part the inspirer and the creator. Yet the Roman Catholic tie not only did not retain the Greek East: it also was not as strong as Armenian, Egyptian, and Syrian national feeling. The Gregorian (Armenian), Coptic (Egyptian), and Jacobite (Syrian) churches broke away from it. Nor could it bridge the hostile gulf between Romans and Persians, for in the realms of the latter the Nestorians went their independent way. When northwestern Europe began to approach what might be called cultural maturity and experienced that fresh burst of religious life which we call Protestantism, the Roman Catholic Church proved too inflexible to retain it and henceforth became increasingly identified with that portion of Europe which was Latin (Roman) in culture.

It has been in Latin Europe that the Roman Catholic Church has always had its chief strength and from Latin Europe it has had its main geographic expansion. It has been among those peoples which were most nearly assimilated to Rome that the chief theologians, most of the saints, almost all the religious orders, and the large majority of the missionaries of the Roman Catholic Church have had their origin.

The phenomenal geographic extension which the Roman Catholic Church has had in the past four hundred and fifty years has been closely associated with the peoples of south-western (or Latin) Europe. The great missions of the sixteenth, seventeenth, and eighteenth centuries were largely in conjunction with the colonial enterprises of Spain, Portugal, and France. More of the Roman Catholic missionaries of the nineteenth century were from France than from any other country, and France was then building a new colonial empire. The vast accessions to the Roman Catholic white population in Latin America through migration have been predominantly from Latin Europe. On the other hand the Roman Catholic immigrants to Canada, Australia, and New Zealand have been chiefly from Ireland, which, of course, is not part of Latin Europe. Irish, Germans, and Poles constitute a large proportion of the Roman Catholic population of the United States, and also are not Latin. But the Roman Catholic Germans were mainly from the part of Germany that had been within the borders of the Roman Empire, and a very substantial percentage of the later Roman Catholic immigration to the United States has been from Italy.

The rapid decline of southwestern Europe in the present century as a major force in history, a decline which bids fair to be permanent, bodes ill for the future of the Roman Catholic Church. That church will probably continue to grow, but not as rapidly as in the past four-and-a-half centuries. The increase of Christianity as a factor in the life of the planet is more and more through Protestantism.

Even within its own fellowship the Roman Catholic Church has not achieved true Christian unity. Behind the façade of its ecclesiastical structure, outwardly so impressive, tragic divisions have been present and are still to be seen. If Christian unity is one of love, in which the disciples are one as Christ and the Father are one, the Roman Catholic Church has not achieved it. This we must say sadly, for here is no cause for gloating on the part of the critics of that great church. Jealousies among the bishops, bitter controversies between the religious orders, and cleavages along national lines have been chronic.

Let it be reiterated, the Roman Catholic method of achieving real unity among Christians has proved a failure. It is not thus that the dream of the New Testament is to be realized. The experiment has been ennobled by the labors and prayers of some of the choicest spirits that the world has known, but the centuries are demonstrating that Christian unity must be sought through other channels.

Nor, until the past century and a half, have the other Christian fellowships succeeded any better than has the Roman Catholic Church in propagating the Christian faith throughout the world and in realizing a comprehensive Christian unity. Indeed, their record has not been as good.

Except by emigration the Orthodox churches have scarcely spread outside their own countries. The one exception has been the Russian Orthodox Church. With state aid under the czars it enjoyed something of an extension among non-Russian peoples and regions within the Russian Empire. Yet outside that empire it had only three small missions among non-Christians—in Japan, China, and Alaska—and the last named was begun when Alaska was part of the empire.

Moreover, the Orthodox churches are at best only a loosely united family. Most of those in Europe are national churches subordinate to their respective governments. In theory they meet together in ecumenical councils, but centuries have elapsed since one of these has been held which has the recognition of all the family. Theoretically the Ecumenical Patriarch has a kind of priority, much as that which the Archbishop of Canterbury possesses within the

Anglican communion, but he now exercises direct juris-
diction only over a few thousand of the faithful and but
little recognition is given him by the other Orthodox bodies.
To be sure, a community of faith and practice exists among
the Orthodox churches. A real even if vague and limited
unity exists, but administrative rifts are seen which are
symptomatic of deeper rifts of the spirit.

Nor have the Orthodox displayed much of either initiative or success in attempting to draw other Christians into
an all-embracing unity. The recent return of the Ru-
thenian Uniates to Orthodoxy has been from political rather
than Christian motives—as was the original secession from
Orthodoxy. Here and there a few Christians from other
communions have joined one or another of the Orthodox
churches, but they have been few and uninfluential.

The other Eastern churches have long been quiescent
and have done almost nothing to spread their faith, either
among non-Christians or among other bodies of Christians.
This is understandable, for most of them have been sur-
rounded by Moslem communities in Moslem states where
both law and social pressure have prevented conversions.
Until recently the Syrian Church in South India was con-
tent to remain on the defensive in a Hindu environment,
as a kind of separate caste. Latterly, because of contact
with other Christians, notably the Anglicans, a few of its
members have reached out to non-Christians, but the elements which were most responsive to the Anglican example
found themselves constrained to break away from the majority into a new schism, the Mar Thoma Church.

By its nature Protestantism has been the most divided of
all the main branches of the Christian Church. Two of its
basic distinctive principles, salvation by faith and the
closely related corollary, the priesthood of all believers,
have made for great variety, for if each Christian has direct

access to God by faith and believes himself to be guided by Him without the intermediary of other Christians, differences in experience and belief are certain to develop and to be held tenaciously as of divine inspiration. Until the last hundred and fifty years the record of Protestantism was one of progressive division. Attempts to bring Protestants together in some kind of unity either failed completely or had only incomplete and transitory success. Moreover, during the first two-and-a-half centuries of its history, Protestantism showed very little inclination to spread the Christian faith throughout the world. Except for the thirteen British colonies which clung somewhat precariously to the eastern seaboard of North America and for a few small colonies elsewhere, it was confined almost entirely to northwestern Europe and the British Isles. Its few missions among non-Occidentals had attracted only a few thousand converts.

In the nineteenth century a reverse from this discouraging course began to be seen. Christianity, and especially Protestant Christianity, displayed an expansion which for geographic extent was unprecedented either in its own history or that of any other religion. Through Protestantism Christians around the world began to come together.

Christian communities now arose in almost every island, land, tribe, and nation. Much of this was by migration of professedly Christian folk to the Americas, Australia, New Zealand, and South Africa. However, much was also through accessions from non-Occidental peoples.

Obviously this spread of Christianity was closely associated with the equally remarkable expansion of Occidental peoples and their culture which was one of the most striking features of that amazing century. Christianity was the traditional faith of the Occident. The words "Christendom" and "Occident" were almost interchangeable. At first thought it was to be expected that Occidental peoples would carry their religion with them and that non-Occidental peoples, impressed by the power of the Occident, would adopt much of the culture of the Occident and would accept Christianity as a part of that culture. That had often, indeed usually, been the record in the expansion of other high cultures: religion had been taken over, along with the other aspects of those cultures. It had previously been the record of Christianity: where professedly Christian peoples had gone as conquerors among peoples of a simpler culture the conquered had tended to adopt Christianity. Or where, as was the case during the breakup of the Roman Empire and the Norse invasions, conquering peoples of a lower culture settled as rulers among a majority of a higher culture who were Christian, they took over the faith of the conquered along with other phases of their culture.

In the nineteenth century the situation was not so simple. Many in the Occident had begun to break with their inherited faith. In general merchants were hostile to Christian missionaries and many diplomatic representatives and colonial officials of Western powers were either cool toward missionaries or were openly antagonistic. Non-Occidental peoples, especially those of the high cultures of the Near East, India, and southeastern and eastern Asia, eagerly appropriated the science, the mechanical appliances, and some of the governmental forms of the Occident but were indifferent or hostile to its traditional religion. The nineteenth- and twentieth-century spread of Christianity came about primarily through earnest missionaries. This was true whether that spread was accomplished through retaining the allegiance of the emigrants from Europe and the British Isles in their new environments or through winning converts from among non-Occidental peoples. These missionaries were a product of a fresh burst of life, unprecedented in its extent and power, in the churches of the Occident. This renewed life was in both the Roman Catholic and the Protestant churches. In the Church of England it took the form not only of the Evangelical Awakening but also of the Catholic revival, the emphasis being upon those features which Anglicanism has in common with the churches that have perpetuated the traditions of the Catholic Church of the Roman Empire.

In the Occident a strange contrast was seen. On the one hand defection from Christianity, either tacit or open, was widespread. Many believed Christianity to be incompatible with modern, especially scientific, methods of increasing man's knowledge and welfare, and regarded it as outworn and even as an enemy of social advancement. On the other hand, in some of the very lands where these tendencies were most marked, the Christian faith displayed fresh vigor.

In the Roman Catholic Church the awakening strengthened the old religious orders and gave birth to more new orders and societies than had appeared in any one century of the life of the Church. Many of these orders had missions among their objectives. More of the rank and file of the Roman Catholic Church helped in the financial support of missions than ever before.

The awakening was particularly marked in Protestantism. As never before Protestantism became missionary. Proportionately Protestantism spread more rapidly than did the Roman Catholic Church. Much of the migration from Europe and the British Isles to the New World and Australasia was Protestant by heritage and in their new homes the settlers and their children were for the most part gathered into churches. But it was not only through migration of its adherents that Protestantism grew. Protestantism also conducted extensive missions among non-Occidental peoples. The support of missions became the concern not alone of the leadership of the Protestant churches but also of substantial minorities of the rank and file of the membership. Indeed, numbers of the Protestant churches considered themselves as missionary societies. In many ways the nineteenth and twentieth centuries have been the Protestant centuries. Increasingly the main stream of Christianity has flowed through Protestantism.

In the twentieth century, and especially since 1914, the Christianity thus propagated through the enhanced vigor of the churches of the Occident has become rooted in non-Occidental peoples. No longer is Christianity nearly exclusively Occidental in membership and leadership. For the first time in its history, and, indeed, in the history of any religion, Christianity is becoming really world wide. While mankind, and especially the Occident, has been torn by the world wars of the present century, Christianity has been spreading, unobtrusively but rapidly. In the third of a century after 1914 the number of Christians more than doubled in China and India, the two largest population centers of Asia, and multiplied at least four- or fivefold in Africa south of the Sahara. In the same period the Christian population more than doubled in Indonesia and increased markedly in the islands of the Pacific.

Even more significant than the numerical growth has been the fashion in which indigenous leadership has emerged. Until 1914 the new Christian communities were largely controlled by Occidentals. After 1914 a mounting proportion of the clergy and of the staffs and administrative heads of Christian institutions such as hospitals and schools have been non-Occidentals. This has been marked among both Roman Catholics and Protestants. Roman Catholics have stressed recruiting and training an

indigenous priesthood. In this they have had striking success. Some native priests have been raised to the episcopate.
All the Roman Catholic bishops in Japan and a large proportion of the bishops in China, Indo-China, and India are
now of the native stock. In the 1940's a Chinese bishop was
made a cardinal. In the world gatherings assembled by
Protestants the proportion of non-Occidentals has also
rapidly risen, vivid evidence of the fact that non-Occidental
Protestant Christianity is no longer exclusively Occidental.
In these gatherings non-Occidentals have shown that in
intellectual caliber, breadth of vision, and mature understanding of the Christian faith they are quite the equals of
their fellow delegates from the Occident. It is significant,
moreover, that in these Protestant gatherings the average
age of the non-Occidentals has been less than that of the
Occidentals. Here is proof that the trend to indigenous
leadership in these non-Occidental units of the Protestant
world fellowship has been growing rather than declining.
Particularly noteworthy as evidence of this trend are the
records of the two world conferences of Protestant Christian youth, held in Amsterdam in 1939 and in Oslo in 1947.
In both gatherings non-Occidentals were conspicuous. At
Oslo the non-Occidentals were even more prominent than
at Amsterdam. Negro Africans, Indonesians, Indians, and
Chinese were outstanding for their able participation in the
discussions. The large majority of Christians are still
Occidentals, but non-Occidental Christians are rapidly
increasing and are more and more becoming equal partners
with Occidentals in the world-wide Christian enterprise.

The growing share of non-Occidentals in the life of the
churches has been closely associated with that general revolt of non-Occidental peoples against the domination of
the white race which has been so marked a feature of the
twentieth century. Non-Occidental Christians have writhed

under the taunts of their non-Christian fellows that they are servants of white "imperialists" and therefore traitors to their respective peoples. They have wished to preserve their own self-respect and to win the esteem of their non-Christian neighbors. In this ambition they have been encouraged by many Occidental missionaries. The far-seeing among the latter have been keenly aware that if Christianity is really to be global it must be rooted in every tribe and nation, and that it must be neither Occidental nor non-Occidental, but both. The greatest of early missionaries said that for those who had entered into the new life made possible by Christ the difference between Jews, Greeks, barbarians, and Scythians had been erased. For the realization of this dream "white" missionaries have long been working in the preparation of "non-white" Christians for full participation in the churches.

Christianity has taken the opportunity given by the twentieth-century "revolt of color" to display its true genius. From the dynamic inherent in its very nature it has been bringing forth its distinctive fruits in individuals and groups in almost every people. Only a few of the lands geographically more isolated from the currents of the time, notably Afghanistan, Outer Mongolia, and Tibet, have not displayed them. No other religion has approached Christianity in geographic extent. No ideology, not even democracy or Communism, is as widely represented by organized groups. The vision embodied in the Great Commission has by no means been fully realized but it is much nearer fulfillment than it was a century ago. As one looks back over the comparatively brief centuries since its unpromising beginning, its progress toward consummation is clear.

Fully as striking as the global planting of Christianity and the rootage of the faith among peoples and races the world around have been the new ways in which Christians have been coming together in fellowship. The centuries-long movement toward division has been reversed. No longer is the trend toward more and more rifts in the "seamless robe of Christ." A few fresh rents have appeared. Out of the vigorous life of Protestantism new varieties of that branch of Christianity have come into being. Yet with gathering momentum Christians have been drawing together.

Six features of this movement toward Christian unity, the fulfillment of the prayer "that they all may be one," stand out in striking prominence.

First of all, the movement toward Christian unity has had its origin in that most divided branch of Christianity, Protestantism. It has not been confined to Protestantism. From that branch of the faith and the closely associated Anglican communion it has spread to other major branches of Christianity. It has drawn in some of the Orthodox and other Eastern churches and here and there it has, as yet imperfectly, begun to bridge the gulf between Roman Catholics and non-Roman Catholics. Yet it is still primarily Protestant in its membership.

Second, probably because it has arisen in what is not only the most divided but also the most flexible branch of Christianity, the movement toward unity has many forms and organizational expressions. Some of these follow the traditional patterns by which in the past Christians have sought to achieve unity—through inclusive ecclesiastical structures bound together by common access to the Lord's table, by a written creed or confession of faith, and by a clergy whose services are accepted throughout the united body. More of the visible expressions of the movement toward unity are new, quite without precedent in Christian history. In a great variety of ways Christians are feeling their path toward the unity inherent in their faith. In the novelty of these approaches lies much of the hope of the movement. The old forms of achieving true Christian unity have been proved to be inadequate. If Christians can profit by their records and from them learn what not to do, they will not have been tried in vain. As experiments, some of them successful in particular periods in spreading the faith and in holding large numbers of Christians together, they have contributed to the ongoing Christian stream. Properly appraised, they can yield indications of pitfalls and blind alleys to be avoided in the future.

In the third place, unlike most of its predecessors, the current movement toward Christian unity has not had unity of doctrine or unity of organization as its primary incentive. It has arisen from the purpose of carrying out the Great Commission. Because Protestant Christians have felt the urge and the obligation to proclaim the Gospel and to bring all men to Christian discipleship, they have realized the necessity of coming together for joint planning and action. Believing that the mission to the world can best be accomplished by cooperation across existing ecclesiastical boundaries, they have sought ways of rising above them. This has been a distinct advantage. When the effort to remove differences becomes a primary aim, attention is focused on the causes of division. Debate enters, and even when it is friendly it tends to the more tenacious adherence to convictions conscientiously held.

In the fourth place, the movement toward Christian unity, far from being within the framework of an existing political structure, is transcending existing political boundaries. What was, until the present, the form of organization most nearly successful in bringing all Christians together, the Catholic Church of the third century, grew up, as we have suggested, within the Roman Empire and was in large part dependent on that empire. When the Roman Empire disintegrated, the Catholic Church also broke into fragments which to a large degree corresponded to the ethnic and political divisions which had once been comprised within that empire. We do well to recall, moreover, that the Roman Empire embraced only a small fragment of the earth's surface and only a minority of the population of the globe. The present movement toward Christian unity already extends to more than three fourths of the surface of the globe. It is growing rapidly in an era of the most extensive warfare which mankind has ever known. In a period when the nations of the world have been pulling apart and international chaos is threatened, the Christians of the world are coming together. To some degree the movement is paralleled by such experiences in international government as the League of Nations and the United Nations. Yet its beginnings far antedated these political experiments, and it has gone further, is mounting more rapidly, and is proving more successful than they are. Indeed, it has contributed and is contributing to them.

It is too much to expect that the political and economic unity of mankind will be achieved within the framework and at the instance of a single comprehensive Christian Church which embraces all the human race. That was the ambition of the Roman Catholic Church in the European Middle Ages, an ambition which had only partial realization even in the comparatively small portion of the earth's surface found within the western end of Eurasia and which we know as western and central Europe. No such prospect lies before us for the entire world in any near future. Even after the phenomenal expansion of Christianity in the past century and a half only a minority of mankind are Christians. Moreover, a comprehensive ecclesiastical structure such as was the dream of the great Popes of the

Middle Ages would prove corrupting to the Church and a peril to Christianity. That is one of the lessons of the Middle Ages for later generations of Christians. Yet a different kind of unity, one which is more nearly in accord with the true genius of Christianity, would undoubtedly make for political, interracial, and economic cooperation and harmony throughout the globe.

In the fifth place, this movement for Christian unity is still young and seems to be only in its early stages. Certainly it is still far from complete. As we are to remind ourselves later, it has not yet brought all Protestants together, it has barely begun to attract Orthodox and other Eastern churches, and it has no prospect of drawing into itself the Roman Catholic Church. Yet because during the century and a half of its history it has been gaining momentum and in the past two decades has been growing at an ever-accelerated pace, the probabilities are that it is only in its early beginnings.

Last of all, no one ought now to predict and still less ought any one to attempt to define the precise forms which this movement toward Christian unity will progressively assume. That it will have visible organizational expressions is clear. Unity without these expressions would be impossible. Yet because its forms are so varied and are still so fluid and because it is in its early stages, we cannot now know what manifestations the movement for Christian unity will ultimately take. Indeed, if the unity envisaged in the prayer "that they all may be one" is ever achieved, no organizational expressions will be ultimate. They will always be changing to meet shifting circumstances. If they were ever to become stereotyped and inflexible life would be stifled. Any attempt to confine the ever new wine of the living Gospel within old and therefore inflexible wineskins would mean peril for both.

From these general characteristics we must go on to describe in brief summary the history of the new movement for Christian unity. It is highly significant that the beginnings are to be found in the missionary enterprise. It was the purpose of giving the Gospel to the entire world which first led Christians of diverse ecclesiastical connections to work together. Early in the eighteenth century, not many years after the inception of Protestant missions to non-Occidental peoples, the youthful Society for Promoting Christian Knowledge, Anglican in its constituency and control, began according financial assistance to the Danish Lutheran enterprise in South India. The great British pioneer of missions to non-Occidentals, William Carey, wished all Christians to recognize their responsibility for carrying the Gospel to all the world. He proposed, concretely, that interdenominational conferences to plan the world mission of the Church be held every ten years and that the first should convene in Cape Town in 1810. This suggestion proved too daring for his supporters, but, as we are to see in a moment, eventually conferences of this kind were held, approximately at intervals of a decade. Partly at the instance of Carey, in 1795 the London Missionary Society was formed. In it at the outset were individuals from several denominations and one of its early statements declared that its purpose was not to send abroad any form of church government, but only "the Gospel of the Blessed God." Its sister society, the American Board of Commissioners for Foreign Missions, begun in 1810, for many years had missionaries and supporters from more than one denomination. The British and Foreign Bible Society, organized in 1804, with the purpose of circulating the Scriptures in the British Isles and other countries, drew its governing body and its financial support from members of both the Church of England and non-conformist bodies.

Similarly the American Bible Society, founded in 1816, included members of several denominations.

Missionaries working in individual countries or regions found cooperation necessary across denominational lines for the effective prosecution of their tasks and began assembling in interdenominational conferences. In the second half of the nineteenth century gatherings of this kind became common in India and China. After World War I national Christian councils representative of the majority of the missions and the indigenous churches came into being in many lands and regions, including India, China, Japan, and the Near East. These councils took on more and more functions and through them Christians from many denominations, both native and foreign, worked together and in so working grew in reciprocal understanding and trust.

Similarly in the Occident the missionary forces formed nation-wide interdenominational bodies for cooperative action. In 1893 the Foreign Missions Conference of North America was organized and eventually drew into its membership most of the foreign missionary societies of the United States and Canada. In 1908 the Home Missions Council was formed to plan comprehensively for the United States. In 1912 the Conference of Missionary Societies of Great Britain and Ireland was constituted. Kindred bodies sprang up in several other countries and regions from which missionaries were sent.

Interdenominational cooperation has been achieved among Protestants on a world scale for carrying out the Great Commission. The years 1878 and 1888 saw international interdenominational missionary conferences in London. A still larger one convened in New York in 1900. This last adopted the name Ecumenical Missionary Conference "because the plan of campaign which it proposes covers the whole area of the inhabited globe." By this time the tradition had been established, unconsciously on the pattern of William Carey's dream, that gatherings of this kind should be held every ten years. At Edinburgh in 1910 a still further and very important step was taken. In succession to the earlier decennial gatherings a World Missionary Conference assembled. However, in contrast with its predecessors, attendance at which was by all who cared to come and who in no sense officially represented their respective churches, the Edinburgh gathering was a delegated body. That is to say, the members were officially appointed by missionary societies. The conference, moreover, appointed a Continuation Committee, with the extraordinarily able John R. Mott as chairman. Under Mott's leadership Continuation conferences were held in several lands on the eve of World War I. That struggle brought a postponement of plans for a consummation of the work of the Continuation Committee, but as soon as was feasible after the end of the conflict what was known as the International Missionary Council was brought into being (1921).

The International Missionary Council has for members national and regional bodies, such as the Foreign Missions Conference of North America, the Conference of Missionary Societies of Great Britain and Ireland, and the various national Christian councils. In 1947 its membership included twenty-six such bodies from all five continents and Australasia, and more were soon to be added. In at least two of these bodies Roman Catholics cooperated for a time. The International Missionary Council has maintained offices in London and New York. Through its secretariat and subcommittees its operations are continuous. Approximately every ten years it has organized world conferences —at Jerusalem in 1928, at Madras in 1938, and at Whitby, Ontario, in 1947. It has become a kind of central planning board for Protestant missions. Through it, during World

War II and its aftermath, many missions were kept going which would otherwise have been discontinued. In 1939, soon after the outbreak of that struggle, it created the Orphaned Missions Fund to care for the German missions, cut off from their supporting constituencies. Later, as the German invasion severed the French, Dutch, Danish, and Norwegian missionaries from their home churches, the Fund found support for them. The first large gift came from Scottish Presbyterian sources. This was symbolic, for it went to support German Lutherans—nationals of an enemy country and of a different communion. Here, in the Christian faith, was a tie which transcended warring national lines and ecclesiastical boundaries. More and more, in the International Missionary Council Occidentals and non-Occidentals are working together on a basis of partnership in full equality. Moreover, in its gatherings some of the traditional barriers between the various bodies of Christians have been weakened. Communion services have been held to which all delegates have been invited and which most delegates have attended, regardless of their denominations. The table of the Lord has become, as never before, a bond of fellowship among Christians of varying ecclesiastical traditions and not, as heretofore, a source and symbol of division.

In many other ways the efforts to carry out the Great Commission have brought Christians together across denominational and national lines. The Sunday School movement, begun late in the eighteenth century, has become a widely used method for teaching children and youth the Christian faith. In the local and national bodies which arose for furthering the Sunday Schools men and women of many denominations cooperated. The World's Sunday School Association, formed in 1907 (since 1947 called the World

Council of Christian Education), was a development from
World's Sunday School conventions, the first of which met
in London in 1889. The Young Men's Christian Associations were inaugurated in London in 1844 for the purpose
of winning young men to the Christian faith and helping
them to develop in it. The World's Alliance of the Young
Men's Christian Associations was formed in 1855. Through
its present World's Committee the Young Men's Christian
Associations are brought together on a global scale. They
have been developed in many lands. Although primarily
Protestant in leadership, they know no denominational
barriers and many of their local units have Roman Catholic
members. Others have Orthodox or Coptic members. Similarly Protestant in origin and leadership but broadly inclusive in membership are the Young Women's Christian
Associations. In 1895, largely at the instance and under
the guidance of John R. Mott, through most of his life an
officer of the Young Men's Christian Association, the
World's Student Christian Federation came into being. It
has for its purpose "winning the students of the world to
Christ . . . building them up in Him, and . . . sending
them out into the world to work for Him." It is made up of
national bodies of Christian students and, although primarily Protestant in membership and leadership, in some of
its local units Roman Catholics and Orthodox are to be
found. The World's Student Christian Federation and the
various student Christian movements associated with it
have brought together in their formative years young men
and women from different communions and have accus-
tomed them to common work and worship. Out of them has
come a large proportion of the leadership for the other
movements of the nineteenth and twentieth centuries
through which Christians have cooperated. Similarly the

World's Christian Endeavor Union, organized in 1895, drew into fellowship young people from many different denominations.

What are known as federations or councils of churches have multiplied, especially in the twentieth century. Most of these are local, confined to a single city or state. Others are national. A large proportion of them are in the United States, partly because here a greater variety of churches is found than in any other country and partly because the absence of a state church places all Christian bodies on a basis of legal equality and encourages collaboration. This movement had precursors in suggestions in the first half of the nineteenth century, including especially the *Fraternal Appeal to the American Churches* and *Overture to Christian Union* by an American Lutheran, S. S. Schmucker. Preparatory also was the Evangelical Alliance, founded in London in 1846. This was frankly Protestant and its creation was stimulated by the rise of the Oxford (Anglo-Catholic) movement in the Church of England. It was international and planned for national and regional branches. Dr. Schmucker had proposed what was in essence a federation of churches, but the Evangelical Alliance was not made up of official representatives of the churches but of individuals from many different churches. However, it dreamed of Christian unity and by bringing together outstanding men from different communions it trained them in thinking in larger terms than their respective denominations and cemented friendships across denominational barriers. After further preparatory movements, in 1908 the Federal Council of the Churches of Christ in America was constituted. By 1948 its membership embraced religious bodies which had slightly more than half of the Protestant church membership of the United States. In it as well were the United Church of Canada and three non-Protestant bodies, American branches of Orthodox churches. Its purpose has been "united service for Christ and the world," the promotion of the spiritual life of the churches, and "the application of the law of Christ in every relation of human life." It has been, then, for the joint implementation of the Great Commission by the churches. Its activities have grown with the years. The British Council of Churches, formed in 1942, embraces in its membership the Church of England, the Church of Scotland, and most of the Free churches. It is, therefore, an organ of the overwhelming majority of the non-Roman Catholic churches of the British Isles. Other similar bodies exist in several countries. The most comprehensive of these councils of churches is the World Council of Churches, of which we are to say more in the next chapter. Its constitution was drafted in 1938 but because of the intervening World War II its official formation was delayed until the summer of 1948.

A natural phase of promoting Christian unity has been the bringing together for fellowship of the different branches of the same communion. Thus in the Lambeth conferences, the first of which convened in 1867, the bishops of the Anglican communion have periodically assembled. Similarly the nineteenth and twentieth centuries have seen the formation of world organizations for Baptists, Methodists, Congregationalists, Lutherans, and Reformed churches holding the Presbyterian system.

A phase of the movement for Christian unity which seeks that goal through traditional procedures has been church union. It endeavors to bring two or more churches together into one new ecclesiastical structure. Sometimes this means the coalescence of different branches of the same denominational family. Thus in 1932 the Methodist Church in England was formed by the union of the Wesleyan Methodists, the Primitive Methodist Church, and the United Methodist

Church, and in 1939 the Methodist Episcopal Church, the Methodist Episcopal Church South, and the Methodist Protestant Church coalesced to form the Methodist Church. In 1917 and 1918 the United Lutheran Church came into being through the merger of three Lutheran bodies in the United States. Often unions of different denominations have been formed. Most of these unions have been in lands where the Church is comparatively young and where ecclesiastical lines have not become as inflexible as in lands where it is older. Yet some have been in European countries where upheavals in the environment have weakened old patterns. Most of the unions have had as a dominant motive the more effective carrying out of the Great Commission in their respective environments. Thus the United Church of Canada, formed in 1925 by the union of Methodists, Presbyterians, and Congregationalists, had back of it the conviction that the rapidly expanding communities of the Canadian West could be better reached by the Gospel through collective rather than separate action. In 1925 the Church of Christ in China was constituted with a Presbyterian nucleus. Eventually many former Congregationalists, Baptists, Methodists, and United Brethren joined it. In 1941 the Church of Christ in Japan brought together the large majority of the Protestants of that land. The Church of South India, inaugurated in 1947 after long negotiations, was made up of former Anglicans, Congregationalists, Presbyterians, Methodists, and Reformed. As the twentieth century has worn on, the numbers of these unions have mounted rapidly.

The nineteenth and twentieth centuries have seen friendly approaches between divergent churches, some of them with union in the immediate future as the objective, and some with that as the ultimate hope but not as an early possibility. Thus in the 1880's the Protestant Episcopal Church, followed by the entire Anglican communion through the third of the Lambeth conferences, proposed to other churches a basis for union, revised and modified in 1920, embodying four principles which came to be known as the Lambeth Quadrilateral. Anglicans, some of them bishops, have long been making contacts with the Orthodox and other Eastern churches in an attempt at fellowship and reciprocal understanding.

Here, then, is a multiform and mounting movement to bring about Christian unity. Unlike anything before it in Christian history, it is gathering momentum in an age when the world, torn by strife and threatened with even more destructive conflicts, is in peculiarly desperate need of a spiritual and moral undergirding which will be common to all peoples and nations.

## II

### *The Present Status*

WHAT is the present status of the world Christian
community whose rise and growth we have so
rapidly sketched? We have seen the fashion in
which, for the first time, Christianity is becoming world
wide and is rooted not only in the Occident but also among
practically all non-European peoples. This has been accomplished by both Roman Catholics and Protestants. Both of
these wings of the Christian churches have been growing
among non-Occidental peoples in the past hundred and
twenty-five years, but proportionately Protestants have increased more rapidly than have Roman Catholics. We have
also summarized the process by which, after centuries of
progressive division, Christians have begun to come together. We have pointed out that the new movement toward
Christian unity has come through the most divided wing of
Christianity, Protestantism, and that it has been chiefly
an outgrowth of the effort to win all mankind to the Christian faith and to make that faith dominant in every aspect
of the life of the human race. We must now turn to a description of the situation as it is today and point out the
weaknesses and the strength of the emerging world Christian community.

Any picture of the current situation will be partly out of
date before it can be put into type. The present becomes the
past and the contemporary becomes history even while they
are being recorded. Yet we must seek to capture and to
understand this passing present. Seen against the background of its historical development it gives us a clue to

the direction which the stream of events is taking. By viewing it as a whole and by discerning its present limitations and achievements we can more intelligently form our attitude toward it and direct our action.

First of all, we must again remind ourselves that in spite of as grave threats as that faith has ever faced, when the total global scene is viewed, Christianity is gaining ground. This is true numerically. Here and there in the present century grave losses have been seen. These have been notable in Russia, Turkey, Egypt, and Iran, but they have also occurred, although less spectacularly, in Germany, France, and, probably, in Great Britain. Yet, as we saw in the last chapter, striking gains have been made in non-Occidental lands. In the United States, too, the proportion of the population who are church members has continued the increase which has been one of the significant features of the religious life of the country for at least a century. Moreover, it now seems that in some lands in Europe the numerical swing is again upward. Such appears to be true in Russia. Both the Orthodox Church in that great land and the Evangelical groups akin to the Baptists of Britain and the United States are beginning to recoup the losses which they suffered during the first years after the Revolution of 1917. In Great Britain the churches appear to have turned the corner and to be on the way up. Some of the outstanding intellectuals, such as C. S. Lewis and T. S. Eliot, have become convinced and outspoken Christians. The suggestion has been made that as the defection of the intellectuals from Christianity in the nineteenth century preceded that of the masses, so in the twentieth century the return of the intellectuals may be a prelude to the reconversion of the masses. A splendid lot of young men, carefully screened, returning from the armed services, are preparing for the priesthood of the Church of England. The Free churches of England seem to have an able body of candidates for their ministries. Encouraging experiments have been made in reaching the unchurched, such as the industrial chaplaincies and the Commando campaigns of 1947. The Iona movement is evidence of vigorous life in the Church of Scotland. In Jugoslavia the disestablishment of the Orthodox Church by the new political regime seems to have been accompanied by increased support of the Church by the laity and a sufficient number of aspirants for the priesthood. In China, in spite of the distresses of the past troubled decade brought by foreign invasion and civil strife and of losses in some areas, the churches appear to have increased in numbers. In at least two cities where the flight of a large part of the population to escape the Japanese occupation badly depleted the churches, enough accessions came from the Chinese who remained—many of them poverty-stricken—to fill the gaps. Those Christians who left the eastern coast for the west of China greatly strengthened the Christian forces in the areas in which they took refuge.

In leadership World War II brought grave losses. In Great Britain, much of the continent of Europe, China, and Japan, theological schools and theological departments of universities were badly depleted or even completely suspended. The libraries and physical equipment of some were destroyed. In China and Indonesia numbers of the clergy perished through hardship, overwork, or outright execution. In many lands, in both the Occident and the non-Occident, clergy and laity have suffered from fatigue and undernourishment. Yet in most of these lands the deficiencies are beginning to be made good.

He would indeed be blind who did not recognize that Christianity is by no means universal and that powerful rivals are either growing or are as yet but little weakened. The numerical gains of Christianity among non-Occidentals have been predominantly among animists or near-animists, in other words, those of primitive or near-primitive cultures. Relatively few converts have been drawn from the high religions. The rapid advances in the islands of the Pacific and Africa south of the Sahara have been entirely among animistic folk. In Indonesia the overwhelming majority of the Christians have come from the animistic peoples, while very few have been drawn from the Moslems who form the majority of the population. Only a few thousand converts have been made from Islam, even when those in North Africa, western Asia, Iran, India, Malaya, and Indonesia are taken together, and these have probably been more than offset in numbers by the losses by massacre or by conversion to Islam from the older churches in Egypt, Turkey, and Iran in the past third of a century. Islam is still intact. Except for Spain, Portugal, and Sicily, reclaimed centuries ago, the ground that it won in the early years from Christianity has never been regained. Today Islam, supported by heightened Arab consciousness and nationalism, is showing renewed vigor in Egypt, Indonesia, India, and much of western Asia. The rapid growth of Christianity in India has been almost entirely by an excess of births over deaths and by accessions from the depressed classes and the hill tribes, elements of the population which are little or not at all removed from the primitive stage. The castes, and especially the higher castes, dominant in Indian life, have been only slightly affected. The substantial and growing Christian minorities in Burma are mainly from the Karens and other near-primitive tribes and not from the ruling Buddhist Burmese. The slight numerical strength of Christianity in Siam is due primarily to the hold of Buddhism on that land.

We must also remind ourselves that Communism, which declares that all religion, including especially Christianity, is the opiate of the people, is still spreading. To many, especially among the youth who are to shape the future, it appears to be a much better way to achieve an ideal world than does Christianity. Indeed, a few Christians from the Occident and the non-Occident have exchanged their faith for Communism under the conviction that the latter is a quicker way of obtaining the good life for the masses than is Christianity.

Quite as serious, although not always so overt a threat to Christianity, is the exaggerated nationalism of the age. In the form and intensity in which we have known it in the present century, nationalism is comparatively new. Older than Communism, it is like it in having its origin in the Occident and from there has spread throughout the world. It has been accentuated by the wars of the present century. Claiming as it does the primary allegiance of its citizens, the national state has in fact, although often in hidden fashion, placed itself above God and has sought to make religion a tool to achieve its own ends. The threat is to be seen not only in lands under totalitarian and openly non-Christian governments, but also in countries where the government pays lip service to Christianity.

Permeating much of the world is the less spectacular but even more dangerous secularism. Discounting all religion and putting its faith in science, the machine, man's intellect, and man's aesthetic sense, having no hope in a future life or finding it through a non-Christian spiritualism, the secular temper, highly developed in the Occident, has spread to the non-Occident. For many affected by it, nationalism and Communism have become substitutes for religion. Others, quite aimless, with remnants of ethical standards inherited from religious ancestors, are spiritually and morally adrift, intent upon seizing as much enjoyment as possible from the present. Numbers of them, humanists, have a keen appreciation of art, music, and literature, are eager to see these phases of civilization spread widely among the masses, and wish more education, in terms of the intellect, for themselves and others. Yet they ignore Christianity. Secularism is spreading, not only in the Occident but also in many other parts of the world.

However, all is not well with the traditional rivals of Christianity. One of the greatest of them, Confucianism, is rapidly crumbling and is leaving a vacuum in the great land which it once dominated. It has shown no marked creative vigor since the twelfth or thirteenth century and its two chief supports, the Confucian Empire and the educational system associated with that empire, perished in the early part of the present century, victims of their own decrepitude and the invasion of the Occident. Taoism, a minor but once influential Chinese religion, now long decadent, has also been disintegrating under the pressure of new ideas from the West. In Japan the state phase of Shinto, the close associate of Japanese nationalism and imperialistic ambition, has been disestablished by order of the forces of occupation, and its weakened condition has left a void which is not yet filled. For at least a thousand years Buddhism has been slowly waning. Not since the fourteenth and fifteenth centuries, when it won the Mongols, has it made significant territorial gains. Several hundred years ago it died out in India and is now represented in the land of its birth only by immigrant populations. For at least nine centuries it has been declining in China and it has also been decaying in Korea. Between five and six hundred years ago it was displaced in Java by Islam. Although still strong in Japan, it has there long been on the defensive. Not since the thirteenth and fourteenth centuries has Buddhism given rise to any significant new movement in any land. Hinduism still prevails in most of India, but except for the island

of Bali it has lost all the ground which it once held among
non-Indian peoples. One of its closest observers, perhaps
with a foreshortening of history, declares it to be a massive
ruin. Certainly many modern Indian nationalists with
Western training regard it, along with all religions, as an
enemy of the united India for which they long and would
gladly see it abandoned. The religious element is gradually
being dissolved from the Jewish communities. Even Islam,
six centuries younger than Christianity and at one time its
doughtiest opponent, has lost ground to nationalism and
secularism: the regime which has been in power in Turkey
during most of the present century regards it with un-
friendly eye and has placed restrictions on it. Much of the
renewed vigor of Islam in Egypt, Arabia, Iraq, and Pales-
tine is due more to Arab nationalism than to inherent religious conviction. The creation of Pakistan is not so much
from the religious enthusiasm of the Indian Moslems as
from communal solidarity and the fear of discrimination
from the Hindu majority.

Even the younger current competitors of Christianity
are not immune to serious weaknesses. Communism is clearly
inadequate to accomplish even what it professes to do. In
Russia it has not freed man but has further enslaved him.
The Revolution of 1917 which brought the Communists
into power has meant the substitution of one police rule by
another. Instead of the czar and the old aristocracy with its
bureaucracy, army, and secret police there is a new aristocracy, not hereditary, but made up of the leaders of the
Communist party and certain professional groups which
the party favors. The army and the bureaucracy have persisted, although with different personnel and organization,
and the secret police are more effective in suppressing dissent than under the czars. Basically, moreover, the view

which Communism holds of the nature of man, the universe, and history is so far from the truth that it is hard to see how it can endure. To anyone familiar with the facts and not blinded by emotion it is clear that the excessive nationalism of our time, with its emphasis upon the sovereign state, is fraught with disaster. It is the major obstacle to the economic and political cooperation of mankind that has been made imperative by the mechanical inventions which by annihilating distance are rendering the entire human race ever more interdependent. Unless nationalism can be transcended by increasing cooperation, major disasters are in store. Secularism is more elusive, more multiform, and more difficult to meet than are Communism and nationalism, but it can never satisfy the deepest hungers of men's hearts.

These weaknesses do not mean that the rivals of Christianity for the allegiance of mankind will be overcome either easily or quickly. But it is evidence of its vitality that in spite of the strength of its competitors Christianity has spread so widely and continues to spread. From both its record and its nature, Christianity rather than its competitors is to rule the future.

Not only is Christianity growing numerically. It is touching the life of mankind more broadly than ever before. In the last chapter we noted the fashion in which Christianity is no longer so nearly exclusively Occidental, but in leadership is becoming ever more deeply rooted among non-Occidental peoples the world around. That process is continuing. In addition, Christianity is affecting more or less profoundly the lives of almost all peoples.

The multitudinous contributions of Christianity to the Occident are well known. Although none has been brought into complete conformity with it, every aspect of the culture of the Occident has long borne the impress of Christianity. Schools and universities, hospitals and institutions for orphans and the aged, marriage, the family, the rearing of children, standards of morals both private and public, democratic ideals, law, art, architecture, music, and literature, all in one way or another and to a greater or less extent are the products of Christianity or have been influenced by it.

In the past few decades Christianity as a stimulating and molding force has been making itself felt among almost all non-Occidental peoples. During the past century and a half more languages have been reduced to writing under the impulse of Christianity than by all other factors in all the history of mankind. Christian schools and hospitals have been founded among people after people. In spite of the difficulties of the late war and its aftermath, most of them are still maintained, or, if destroyed in the hostilities, are being restored. In China the foundations of the modern medical and nursing profession and of public health were the work of Christians and today institutions of Christian origin have a major part in their maintenance and continued growth. Through Sun Yat-sen, a confessed adherent of that faith, Christianity has had a share in shaping the ideals of the revolutions which have transformed the political face of China. Through Gandhi who, although a Hindu and not a Christian, willingly acknowledged his debt to Jesus, Christianity has been a factor in molding the new India. Also, through its contribution to the emancipation of women and to the bettering of the lot of the depressed classes, Christianity is to some degree responsible for the India of today. In land after land much the same kind of story could be repeated with variations. Even in western Asia, where the number of Christian communities has waned in the present century, the influence of Christianity, although impossible of accurate measurement, has undoubtedly increased in the past two or three decades through the work of hospitals, schools, and other institutions.

The very distresses brought on by the wars of our day have been the occasion of a world-wide demonstration of the characteristic genius of Christianity, a demonstration which for geographic extent and magnitude is without precedent in the history of Christianity or of any other religion. Relief to sufferers from the war and its aftermath given directly or indirectly through the churches is more extensive than anything of the kind which the churches have previously accomplished. To the Christian relief agencies contributions have come from individuals, groups, and congregations in many different lands. The relief has been administered in scores of the islands of the sea and on all the continents except possibly South America. The widespread work of the Friends Service Committees, while in the name of the Quakers and directed by them, has drawn a large proportion of its funds and personnel from the membership of many other Christian bodies. It is, in a sense, another expression of the growing Christian unity which is so marked a feature of our day. So, too, Church World Service has been the agency for American Protestant Christians of many different denominations and has sent across the Atlantic and the Pacific millions of dollars and thousands of tons of materials for relief and reconstruction. From its Geneva office the World Council of Churches has channeled much of this relief to the countries of Europe. The Orphaned Missions Fund of the International Missionary Council continues to aid distressed Protestant missions regardless of their nationality or denomination. While by no means officially connected with the churches, the Red Cross by its very symbol discloses the part which Christianity plays in its widespread ministry to human suffering both in war and in peace. So, too, much of the relief through private agencies and by individuals, such as the CARE packages, has been by Christians who have been moved by their faith. From the Christians of Great Britain, although impoverished by war, aid has gone to peoples in the devastated lands of Europe, and in stricken China Christians have given out of their poverty for relief to sufferers about them. In France, CIMADE, frankly Christian, has been of great use to dislocated and impoverished youth, and the French Interchurch Aid Committee has through funds and goods collected in France eased the sufferings of many.

Less clear is the part of Christianity in stimulating the relief given through governmental channels. For magnitude this relief is far beyond any precedent. Most of it has come from the United States. It has been administered partly through UNRRA and partly through other programs and agencies, such as ERP, and it has gone not only to the allies of the United States in World War II, but also to peoples who were enemies in that conflict. Much of this relief has been given from political and economic expediency, but no small part of the motive has been altruistic, the unwillingness to stand by in comparative comfort and see the sufferings of other peoples without attempting to alleviate them. Much of this motive is quite certainly Christian in origin.

Christianity has been and is a teacher in building the world government so desperately called for by the international anarchy and the threat of chaos of our day. The League of Nations would not have come into being but for the efforts of Woodrow Wilson, and Wilson was inspired and maintained by his Christian faith. Those who labored to build popular support for the League in Great Britain and America were largely from the churches. By their education of their constituencies and their representations to the President and the Congress, the Christian forces had an important share in bringing the United Nations into being. They also have had a large part in creating popular support for that organization.

Christianity is by no means dominant in the present world. Only a minority profess and call themselves Christians, and a still smaller minority of those who bear the Christian name allow their faith to be the controlling force in their lives. Not yet have all men been made disciples. Still less have they been taught to observe all Jesus commanded his immediate followers. But never has Christianity been as widely influential in the affairs of men as it is now. And that influence is continuing to mount.

What is the present status of the movement to bring all Christians into a world-wide community which will demonstrate the power of their faith to knit men together in love?

Here the task is by no means fully accomplished. Great gulfs continue to exist. The deepest and the widest are between the major families of Christians. The Orthodox churches and the Roman Catholic are no nearer composing their differences than they were a century ago. Indeed, they are farther apart than they were in the fifteenth century, when for a brief time the gap between them appeared to have been closed. Between Protestants and Roman Catholics the gulf appears to be widening. Under the pressure of the common foe, during World War II, fairly extensive cooperation between Roman Catholics and Protestants was seen, notably in Germany. This continues. But in the United States tension between Roman Catholics and Protestants is growing. It has been present since the large influx of the former in the first half of the nineteenth century and has been more intense at some times than at others. The National Conference of Christians and Jews, formed between the two World Wars, attempted to allay it. However, it is again becoming prominent. Moreover, in some localities in Mexico Roman Catholics, partly released from the repressive measures instituted against them by the state in the 1920's and 1930's, have engaged in sharp persecution of Protestants.

Friction between Roman Catholics and non-Roman Catholics is almost inevitable. The Roman Catholic Church honestly and frankly believes that Christian unity can be achieved only within her fold. She recognizes that millions of baptized Christians have not so conformed. Yet by the very fact of their baptism she claims them as rightfully hers. She regards them as belonging to her soul although not to her body. Since she holds herself to be by Christ's commission the only true church and views all other churches as in error, she cannot conscientiously cooperate with them on the basis of equality. Any collaboration with Christians or bodies of Christians outside her communion must be, from her standpoint, less than ideal. To be consistent she must regard all toleration of such bodies as a necessary evil and must seek to win over their members. Naturally the Orthodox churches and Protestants cannot accede without sacrificing their separate existence and what they believe, just as conscientiously, to be their divinely appointed mission. They must, too, regard Roman Catholics as in error and at most only tolerate that error.

Here and there individual Roman Catholics and non-Roman Catholics can and do establish friendly relations and even find in their common allegiance to Christ a bond which leads to a deep community of spirit. Occasional groups can do so informally. Thousands of Protestants have nourished their devotional life on such Roman Catholic classics as the *Imitatio Christi* and Augustine's *Confessions*. Many Roman Catholic hymns, notably the *Te Deum*, are employed in Protestant worship. Protestant theologians are familiar students of the great Roman Catholic formulations of the faith, such as those of Augustine and Thomas Aquinas. In this fashion a tie is maintained.

Yet from the Roman Catholic viewpoint Protestantism at best has only part of the truth and owes to its Roman Catholic heritage such of the Gospel as it retains. Half a loaf may be better than no bread, and Protestantism is to be preferred to secularism or atheism. But the conversion of Protestants is to be desired and any attempt of Protestants to win Roman Catholics must be rejected. The Roman Catholic hierarchy, for instance, has bitterly resented Protestant missions to Latin America on the ground that the latter is a Roman Catholic region. Under such conditions, tension between Roman Catholics and non-Roman Catholics, while at some times and places quiescent, is always at least latent and occasionally breaks out into open hostility.

The old divisions among the Eastern churches persist. Orthodox and Jacobite, Armenian and Orthodox, and Jacobite and Nestorian are still separated by the issues which have held them apart from the beginning.

Protestants and the Eastern churches also know friction. Protestant missions have led to schisms in these ancient bodies, for the conservative majorities have expelled the minorities who, influenced by Protestantism, have sought to bring changes into the mother churches. In some predominantly Orthodox lands, such as Rumania, converts to Protestantism have been persecuted.

Nor is the family of Orthodox churches a unit. Just now a dividing line is drawn between the Orthodox churches in Communist Russia and her satellites on the one hand and on the other the Orthodox churches in those lands which are fearful of becoming subject to Russia. Thus the Ecumenical Patriarch, with his residence in Turkey, and the

Orthodox Church of Greece declined to participate in an all-Orthodox conference called by the Patriarch of Moscow, presumably because they feared that such a conference would be used to further Russian imperialistic ambitions.

In spite of the movement which is bringing Protestants together, Christian unity has not been fully achieved within that branch of Christianity. To be sure, Christians of different denominations are working together as never before and in a growing variety of ways Protestant denominations are cooperating with one another. Yet several denominations, some of them large, decline to work with others. Some denominations, usually younger ones, seek to grow at the expense of the others. Moreover, many of the ultra-conservatives or Fundamentalists look with suspicion upon all "modernist" or "liberal" tendencies. In the United States they place in that category the Federal Council of Churches of Christ in America and city and state federations of churches. Some of them have formed the National Association of Evangelicals and others have constituted the American Council of Christian Churches, for they are not able to agree entirely among themselves. Cleavages exist within individual churches, some of them on matters of policy and doctrine, and others arising from rivalries and friction between strong leaders.

From several angles, the very movement toward Christian unity has multiplied divisions. Thus the Church of England is not in communion with the newly formed Church of South India, although the majority of the latter's members were Anglicans until the new body came into being. More important still, the new bodies through which Protestants are cooperating do not form a consistent pattern and are organizationally not dovetailed into one another. It would be natural to expect that the Federal Council of the Churches of Christ in America would be made up of delegates chosen by the state councils of churches and that they, in turn, would be composed of representatives of city, county, and other local councils. It would seem to be in accord with good organizational procedure to have the World Council of Churches composed of delegates from national councils of churches. Yet the facts are quite the opposite. In America state and city councils of churches are quite independent of one another and the Federal Council of the Churches of Christ in America is directly representative of the national organizations of its member churches and not of state, city, or local councils. Such bodies as the World's Committees of the Young Men's and Young Women's Christian Associations, the World's Student Christian Federation, and the International Missionary Council send representatives to the sessions of the Assembly of the World Council of Churches, but their organizations are not knit into that of the latter. Then, too, when some of these ecumenical gatherings convene, their members find it impossible to hold a common communion service. For instance, no such services were possible at the world conferences of Christian Youth at Amsterdam in 1939 and at Oslo in 1947. In other words the very organizations through which Protestants have sought to work together have seemed to multiply the divisions in that wing of the Christian forces.

Many of the executives of denominational and interdenominational agencies are finding that cooperation has so multiplied the committee and board meetings by which this is being accomplished that they have leisure for little else. At times the organizational structure through which Christian unity is being sought threatens to break down through sheer weight and complexity.

Fortunately this is by no means all the story. The organizations through which Christian unity is being sought are making progress and are more inclusive of the many varieties of Christianity than any which have heretofore been known. Any effort to bring all the churches together in any one of the existing traditional ecclesiastical patterns would be foredoomed. This would seem disloyalty to what the other churches believe to be the truth which has been committed to them. Yet, as we saw in the last chapter, Christians are in fact coming together. In doing so they are displaying an initiative and a vigor which are approached by no other religion and a harmony and a minimum of friction which far surpass any of the intergovernmental organizations of mankind. Harmony is by no means complete nor is friction entirely absent, but the amazing advance registered is evidence of a power within the Christian faith which makes for unity and reciprocal trust.

The seeming confusion, disorder, and variety of approaches toward Christian unity may be an advantage. Were any one organizational pattern to be adopted, the attempt to make and keep it universal would, as in the case of the Catholic Church of the Roman Empire and one of its successors, the Roman Catholic Church, and of many a state church within a particular area, provoke fresh divisions. By allowing freedom the absence of any one organizational pattern has thus far furthered the true unity, that of the spirit.

The most comprehensive of the organizations which is promoting Christian unity is the World Council of Churches. The fashion in which it was brought into being established the precedent for its inclusiveness. It began as a fusion of two existing organizations, the World Conference on Faith and Order and the Universal Christian Council for Life and Work.

The first of these bodies was a direct outgrowth of the World Missionary Conference which, as we saw in the last chapter, was held in Edinburgh in 1910. Those responsible for the program had agreed that the purposes of the gathering, bringing the Gospel to the entire world, could be best accomplished by silence on the historic differences which separated the churches. One of the delegates, Bishop Charles R. Brent of the Protestant Episcopal Church, believed that Christian unity could be achieved only as these differences were frankly faced. At his instance the Convention of the Protestant Episcopal Church unanimously initiated steps to invite "all Churches which accept Jesus Christ as God and Savior to join in conferences following the general method of the World's Missionary Conference, for the consideration of all questions pertaining to the Faith and Order of the Church of Christ." Action was delayed by World War I, but following that conflict a committee of the Protestant Episcopal Church visited the Eastern churches to invite them to cooperate. Several of these bodies accepted. The Pope was also approached but, consistently with the well-known attitude of his church, declared that the only rightful way to unity was submission to him as the Vicar of Christ. In 1927 the Faith and Order Conference met in Switzerland, at Lausanne. To it came official delegates from a very large proportion of the non-Roman Catholic churches, among them not only Protestants and Anglicans, but also several of the Orthodox churches, two of the other Eastern churches, and two of the Old Catholic churches. Lausanne faced frankly the issues which had lain back of many of the divisions among the churches—the faith of the Church, and the nature of the Church, the ministry, and the sacraments. It issued a "message of the Church to the world" which was in reality a statement of faith and which proved that Christians of widely different traditions could agree on the basic convictions of their religion. The Lausanne conference was also a demonstration that common worship was possible and that issues which had long been controversial could be discussed with amity and reciprocal respect even when full agreement was as yet impossible.

The second of the two bodies which joined in the World Council of Churches, the Universal Christian Council for Life and Work, arose out of the desire to obtain "cooperation in testimony and action" in the application of Christian faith and principles to the practical issues of human society, including especially economic and political problems and war and peace. Several organizations in Great Britain and the United States paved the way. The outstanding leader was Archbishop Nathan Söderblom of Sweden. Preparatory, too, was the World Alliance for International Friendship through the Churches, constituted in August, 1914, at a meeting in Constance, Switzerland, which had been planned before the outbreak of World War I. This body was not officially representative of the churches, and membership in it was of individuals. It was primarily Protestant but it also contained some from the Orthodox churches. After a number of preliminary meetings, there assembled in the summer of 1925, at Stockholm, what was called the Conference on Life and Work. Like the Lausanne gathering two years later, the Stockholm conference was representative of a wide variety of churches and included some from the Orthodox. A communion service was held according to the rites of the Church of Sweden at which Archbishop Söderblom was the celebrant and to which all the delegates were invited. In its discussions, fellowship, and common worship, the gathering made for a sense of unity across diverse ecclesiastical boundaries and between the Germans and their late enemies. It also was a stimulus to a growing concern of the churches for the social order.

In 1937 both the Universal Christian Council for Life and Work and the World Conference on Faith and Order again convened, the first at Oxford in July and the second in Edinburgh in August. The Oxford gathering registered a marked advance over Stockholm. Especially was this true in the statement of the attitude of the Church to the State and in the discussion and statement on the vexed question of war and peace. Here, as at Stockholm, a communion service was held for all delegates according to the rite of the established church, in this case the Church of England. At Edinburgh common ground was reached on such historic sources of cleavage as the relation of justification and sanctification and of predestination and free will, with the declaration that the differences were such as no longer to justify division.

As early as 1933 an effort had been made to bring into closer association Faith and Order, Life and Work, the International Missionary Council, the World Alliance for International Friendship through the Churches, the World's Committee of the Young Men's Christian Associations, and the World's Student Christian Federation. This led to a continuing Consultative Committee, and in July, 1937, before the meetings of Life and Work and Faith and Order, an enlarged meeting called by this committee recommended that these two should be merged in a new body to be called the World Council of Churches. The Oxford and Edinburgh conferences approved the project and appointed a joint committee to carry it through.

Accordingly in May, 1938, a representative body chosen by the churches met at Utrecht, in the Netherlands, and drafted a constitution for the World Council of Churches. This body is described in that document as "a fellowship of the churches which accept our Lord Jesus Christ as God and Savior." It is "to carry on the work of the two world movements, Faith and Order and Life and Work, to facilitate common action by the churches, to promote cooperation in study, to promote the growth of ecumenical consciousness in the members of the churches, to establish relations with denominational federations of world-wide scope and with other ecumenical movements, and to call world conferences on specific subjects as occasion may require." The World Council is not to "legislate for the Churches," but it is to "offer counsel and provide opportunity of united action in matters of common interest," and "it may take action on behalf of constituent Churches in such matters as one or more of them may commit to it." The principal authority of the World Council of Churches is an assembly which ordinarily meets once every five years and which has a membership of not more than four hundred and fifty members. There is a Central Committee which meets normally every calendar year.

Because World War II broke out in Europe a little over a year after the World Council of Churches' constitution was drafted, the assembly did not hold its first meeting until the summer of 1948. At that gathering, at Amsterdam, the World Council was formally and officially brought into being. In the meantime it had been functioning with a secretarial staff and with headquarters in Geneva and other offices in London and New York. Through its provisional organization the World Council of Churches helped to keep together the churches across the warring lines of World War II. After that conflict passed, fellowship between Christians on opposite sides of the war, which had never really been broken, was resumed much more easily and quickly than after World War I. After the war, as we have seen, the Geneva office became the center for relief for the Christians and churches of Europe. Through Geneva, moreover, extensive studies were organized through commissions in which Christian scholars of many lands participated in preparation for the first meeting of the assembly. At the

Ecumenical Institute, conducted near Geneva, groups, largely of young people, have come together from many nations and churches for intimate fellowship, study, and worship.

Before the first assembly met, over a hundred and twenty-five churches had joined the World Council. They were found on all five continents, in Australasia, and in the islands of the Pacific. They included many of the "younger churches" of the non-Occident which had arisen from the missions of the "older churches" of the Occident. They also embraced not only churches from the main ecclesiastical families of Protestantism—Lutherans, Reformed, Presbyterian, Anglican, Methodist, Congregational, Baptist, and many others—but also the Old Catholic churches, several of the Orthodox churches (among them the Greek Orthodox Church), the Coptic Church, the Syrian (Jacobite) Church, the Nestorians, and part of the Syrian Church of India. The World Council of Churches also has close ties with the International Missionary Council, the various "world confessional associations," and such ecumenical bodies as the World's Student Christian Federation and the World's Committees of the Young Men's and Young Women's Christian Associations.

The World Council of Churches is thus the most inclusive body that Christianity has ever possessed. Its program embraces not only the fields dealt with by Faith and Order and Life and Work, but also relief to the victims of war and plans for giving the Christian Gospel to the entire world. It officially represents a larger number and a wider confessional and geographic range of Christians than any other organization which the centuries have known. It also provides a center of coordination for the various other organizations in which Christians cooperate on a world scale, whether as individuals or through representatives of the churches. The ties with the International Missionary Council are especially close. For a variety of reasons it seems clear that the International Missionary Council and the World Council of Churches will not coalesce, at least within the next few years. Yet there is much interlocking of personnel: several of the men and women prominent in the one are also prominent in the other. The utmost friendship exists between the two organizations and increasing provisions are being made for close collaboration.

In a variety of ways true Christian unity, that of love, worship, action, and agreement in loyalty to a common Lord, is making rapid progress through the World Council of Churches and the organizations associated with it.

First of all there is a growing awareness that the gulfs which separate Christians are contrary to the genius of their faith and are weakening to the Church's witness. When one ecclesiastical body could dominate a particular country or region, as was true of the Roman Catholic Church in southwestern Europe, of the Church of England in England, of the Church of Sweden in Sweden, and of several of the Orthodox churches in their respective countries, it could place the onus for division upon the minorities which dissented from it. In the present world with its shrinking distances all churches are brought into more or less close contact with one another, whether they are the various state churches, the Roman Catholic Church, the Eastern churches, or the dissenting churches. The disestablishment which has made rapid strides in the present century has deprived church after church of the support and prestige which have accrued from official connection with the state. In the United States all churches are on the basis of legal equality, and those which in the Old World were state churches must rub shoulders with one another and with churches which in no land have had the support of the state.

This is also the case in non-Occidental lands where missions have planted a variety of denominations. The effect has been, except in the most intransigent bodies, to create the conviction that all churches must share in the responsibility for the current divisions and that no one ecclesiastical body has a full-orbed expression of the Christian faith. This feeling of common guilt and of the incompleteness of the witness of any single church has been furthered by the organizations and gatherings in which Christians of various churches have come together.

In the second place, the various bodies which have brought Christians of differing ecclesiastical traditions together have promoted understanding, fellowship, and trust. As they have worked and worshiped together Christians have discovered that their common Christian faith has given rise to a kind of character which all recognize as distinctively Christian, no matter in what church it is found. They discover that all churches produce this character, that it is seldom seen outside the churches, and that even when it is found outside them it reaches its highest development only within the company of one or another of the churches. Even historic differences which have so entered into the warp and woof of religious experience that they seem to be essential to it, when discussed frankly with the desire to understand and to be understood rather than with the purpose of convincing those who disagree, cease to create a breach in this higher and deeper unity.

In the third place, through the association, understanding, and friendships made possible through the many organizations and movements which surpass ecclesiastical and national lines, the faith of those who participate is immeasurably deepened and ennobled. The Christian Gospel is so great that no one statement and no single ecclesiastical tradition, no matter what its value and wealth, can fully express it. Those who have penetrated furthest into the richness of the faith as it has been conveyed to them by a particular church are often the best prepared to appreciate the values which have been found in another church. For instance, one who has meditated long on the meaning of the Cross of Christ and has found some of his highest moments of spiritual insight in the communion service of the denomination in which he has been reared, is the better prepared to appreciate the meanings seen in the Cross and the service of Holy Communion by the finest intellects and souls of other denominations and of traditions quite different from his own. The varieties in the Church Universal, thus shared, make for a richer faith.

In the next place, it is significant that the "ecumenical" contacts are more among the leadership of the various churches than among the rank and file of the membership. That means that they do not arise from indifference to the tenets and practices of the churches. On the contrary they are among those who are most familiar with the doctrines and traditions of their respective churches and who might be expected to have a personal and even a selfish stake in their perpetuation. Indeed, it is a weakness of the movements for world-wide Christian unity that they have thus far been too much confined to the leaders of the various churches and have not yet won the intelligent allegiance of the rank and file of the church membership. Through this leadership the movement will in time penetrate and indeed is already penetrating to those most active in the local congregations and will eventually be appreciated by the majority of Christians. The fact that it has come first among those who have entered most deeply into the heritages of their respective churches and are most concerned that these heritages be preserved gives support to the conviction that in this new trend toward Christian unity we have indications of a fresh burst of life in the world-wide Christian community which may prove to be fully as important as the Protestant Reformation, the Catholic Reformation of the sixteenth century, or the Evangelical Awakening in Protestantism in the eighteenth and nineteenth centuries. Here is no shallow or transient current, but one which is making itself felt through souls most sensitive to the world's needs and to the resources in the Christian Gospel for meeting those needs.

It is hopeful that this movement toward Christian unity is not defensive. It has not arisen as a reaction to the terrors of our time. It is not here because Christians, realizing the threat presented by the present world situation and the many enemies of their faith, are desperately attempting to find strength in a common front. As we reminded ourselves in the last chapter, the movement had its origin in the optimistic nineteenth century when the progress of mankind seemed assured. It came into being because Christians were endeavoring to fulfill the Great Commission and believed that this could be better done through cooperation than through the various denominations working separately. The movement still has obedience to the Great Commission as its major objective. If it were to cease to do so it would become sterile. Confronted by the perils and upheavals of our day, the leadership of the churches is convinced of the urgency of obedience to the Great Commission before chaos engulfs mankind and is pressing forward in a united campaign. But back of this acceleration is not only a sense of urgency, an awareness that the time may be short in which Christians can act: there is even more a confident hope, a hope founded upon the belief that the God and Father of our Lord Jesus Christ is sovereign in the affairs of men and that in Christ He has inaugurated a new order, a society in which His will is acknowledged. That new order was introduced in seeming weakness, the weakness of a babe in a manger, and of a lonely figure on a Roman cross. Yet the Christian faith is that the weakness of God is stronger than men, that God is both power and love, and that the power of that love will ultimately triumph. Indeed, it has already triumphed in the lives of thousands of men and women, most of them obscure, and it is continuing to triumph in the spread of the world-wide Church and in the growing unity in that Church.

# III

## *What of the Future?*

WHAT is to be the future of the world Christian community? Is the Great Commission ever actually to be fulfilled? Will all men everywhere become disciples and observe all that Jesus commanded the little inner group of his immediate followers? What is to be the fate of the non-Christian systems, especially the great historic religions? Will they completely disappear, displaced by Christianity? Is there to be a world-embracing religion which will be a compound of the chief existing faiths? Or is there to be a world-wide Christianity which, while bearing that name and honoring Christ as the supreme revelation of God, will in reality incorporate many of the essential features of its rivals? Will Christianity, triumphant, be a composite of all the insights which men have had into the world of the Spirit? Or will the victorious Christianity perpetuate the original Gospel, purged of compromises with local and national environments, cultures, and competing religions? Will the Christian community embrace all men everywhere and be a realization of the prayer "that they all may be one, even as thou Father art in men and I in thee, that they also may be in us"? If this unity is realized, what will be its visible expressions? Will it be an extension of any one of the ecclesiastical patterns which we know today? Will it, for example, be bound together and have its continuity through the historic episcopate and the apostolic succession? Will it repeat the historic creeds, especially the Apostles' Creed and the Nicene Creed? Will it preserve any of the sacraments and, if so, which? Will it continue to regard the Bible as the inspired word of God? Will the world Christian community present great varieties of organization? Will some of these be regional or national and in part conform to the cultural heritage of their respective environments? Can we forecast with any degree of confidence the eventual structure of this world Christian community?

Obviously these questions are of primary importance. Obviously, too, since they have to do with the uncertain future, we cannot know all the answers. However, we can ascertain some of the facts which will help to determine the answers. From these facts forecasts can be ventured which, while still conjectures, may prove to be not far from the event.

To approach answers we need both insight into the nature of the Christian faith and historical perspective.

Of the very essence of the Christian faith is the conviction that God is sovereign, that He is at work in human history, that His purpose and His nature are revealed uniquely in Jesus, that through Jesus He has achieved man's redemption, and that He has brought into being a community of faith, hope, and love which at once is the body of Christ—the continuation of the Incarnation—and has Christ as its head. The Christian faith declares that God will not be defeated. He has given man a measure of freedom, limited to be sure, but necessary if He is to have not automata but willing sons. Through the misuse of this freedom man may delay the consummation of God's purposes and may cause God to alter the details of His program. Yet ultimately, whether in history or beyond history, God's perfect will is to be accomplished. This is the Christian hope supported by Christian faith.

Historical perspective demands that we think not in terms of decades or even centuries, but of millenniums.

When contrasted with the time which life has existed on the globe mankind is a recent phenomenon. Compared even with the brief span which man has thus far had on the planet, civilization is only a moment. For the most part it has developed since the last retreat of the ice sheets from Europe, Asia, and North America, a period which may be as much as thirty or thirty-five thousand years but which, on the geologic clock, is only a fraction of a second. Moreover, compared even with the few millenniums which have thus far been marked by the presence of civilization, Christianity is a very recent feature of the human scene.

From the fact that Christianity is so new an arrival two contrary predictions are possible. The first would regard Christianity as a transient feature of man's course on this planet. In support of this prophecy is the record of other religions. Religions seem to follow a fairly clearly defined life course. They have their origin, their creative years, and their geographic spread. Then new movements cease to appear within them, their geographic expansion ceases, the communities adhering to the faith dwindle, and eventually the religion disappears. Sometimes this course is brief, as in the case of the mystery religions once so prominent in the Roman Empire. Sometimes it may cover a thousand years or more. This was the record of Manichaeism. That religion began in the third century in Mesopotamia, and eventually reached from western Europe to the China Sea. It then died out. Buddhism, Taoism, and Confucianism have had a somewhat longer life span but have been waning for eight or nine hundred years. Although younger, Islam appears to be going the same way. Judaism persists, but for many centuries it has given rise to no markedly new religious movements and of late years an increasing number of Jews are abandoning the religious elements of their tradition and are becoming purely secular. Jainism continues, but as a minority which has not expanded for many centuries and has long shown no major fresh currents of life. Hinduism is still vigorous, but centuries ago it lost most of such footing as it had acquired outside of India. The inference would be natural that Christianity is to have the same course. It has been closely associated with the Occident, the culture which developed in the basin of the Mediterranean and which, continuing chiefly in Europe after the Arab irruption, has since spread from Europe, chiefly from western Europe and its peoples. If the Occident is declining, the natural inference would be that Christianity is already losing its hold.

The other prediction is that Christianity is still young and that it has only begun its growth. A number of cogent facts give support to this interpretation and forecast. More than any other faith, Christianity has displayed the ability to survive the death of cultures with which it has been intimately associated and, after a period of reverses, to have a striking revival and to go on to fresh advances which carry it beyond its earlier high-water marks. This was its course after the disintegration of the Roman Empire, the state and the culture where it had won its first victories and with which it had become identified. Recovering from that shock, Christianity retained its hold on southern Europe, regained the portions of that continent which it had lost to Islam, won the peoples of northern Europe, and entered more into the civilization of medieval Europe than it had into that of the Roman Empire. When that civilization in turn passed, Christianity was again threatened, but in the awakenings which we call the Catholic and Protestant Reformations it brought the peoples of Europe more nearly to its standards than in the Middle Ages (although they were still far from attaining them), and, accompanying Europeans in their geographical expansion, spread more widely than ever before. The period of the greatest vigor which Christianity has thus far displayed has been the nineteenth and twentieth centuries. This has been in spite of grave threats from new movements in thought and in economic, political, and social life during the greatest period of revolution which the world has ever known, and of dire prophecies of the early demise of the faith. Moreover, as we have reminded ourselves, for the first time in its history or in the history of any other religion, in the present century Christianity has become firmly rooted in almost every people, land, and culture. In spite of the present decline of its original home, western Europe, Occidental civilization continues to spread. Christianity, the traditional faith of the Occident and the inspiration for much of its culture, may be expected to expand with it. By becoming planted, as it has, in every culture, it is in process of achieving independence of Western civilization and is on the way to becoming universal and divorced from any particular culture. The facts of history appear to be on the side of those who declare that Christianity has only begun its life and its growth. It will probably again suffer reverses, possibly as severe as any which it has yet known, but its record gives ground for confidence that if disasters come recovery will follow, and that Christianity will register other advances which will increase its share in the life of mankind.

If this hopeful interpretation of history is corroborated by the future, we may expect Christianity ultimately to be the professed faith of all mankind. This will probably require several thousands of years, but if human civilization and Christianity are still young this ought not to dismay us. It is what we should expect. As we reminded ourselves in the last chapter, even during its great expansion in the past century and a half Christianity has made little headway against the higher religions—Hinduism, Buddhism, and

Islam. These faiths seem to be in slow decline, a decline which in the case of another high religion, Confucianism, has become rapid disintegration. If they continue to wane, Christianity will have an opportunity to fill the vacuum. This, however, may be many centuries hence.

But will all mankind not only be professedly Christian but also be brought into full conformity with the ideals set forth in the teachings of Jesus? Will all men obey all that Jesus commanded the inner company of his friends? If that hope were to be realized, the age of which the seers have dreamed would indeed come. Men would beat their swords into plowshares and their spears into pruning hooks.

The high standard set forth by Jesus and the brevity of human life now seem to preclude the possibility of the attainment of this goal. Jesus commanded his disciples to be perfect as God is perfect. In conformity with this ideal Paul prayed for his fellow Christians that they "might be filled unto all the fullness of God." This was not meant to discourage men by confronting them with a demand which they could not expect to meet. Rather does it hopefully set forth what men are to become if they are to be what God intends them to be. Yet the seven or eight decades which are the far limit of the span of the individual's life are quite too short in which to rise to this expectation. At birth men carry with them a taint from which they cannot be completely purged in so brief a time. It is a basic Christian conviction that life in this body is but a prelude to an endless existence. While here and now men may be born anew and begin the eternal life of growing fellowship with God and likeness to him, within this flesh they do not attain "the goal of the high calling of God in Christ Jesus."

This does not mean that each generation must begin from the same point as did all its predecessors. Real progress is possible. The environments into which men are born may be so improved that it will be increasingly easy for children to develop as Christians. The record of thousands of Christian homes and family lines makes this clear. To be sure, some families slip backward. Many children have failed to carry on the tradition inherited from their parents and in turn to pass it on in full vigor to their children. If he is to know true life each individual must enter it for himself. What has been called "the futility of a second-hand religion" has been demonstrated again and again. Yet first-hand religion is more frequent in a home in which Christian nurture is prominent than where it is absent. Such homes can be multiplied. Indeed, they are being multiplied, even though slowly. Not only is it conceivable that eventually all men will bear the Christian name, but it is also possible that progress will continue to be witnessed on this planet toward the perfection without which man is forever restless and incomplete.

What of the non-Christian religions? Obviously, if all men become Christian they will disappear, even though that event be thousands of years in the future. But will the Christianity of the future be a synthesis of what is now called by that name together with the insights of the systems which it will have displaced? That dream appeals to many. It seems to them ungenerous and even arrogant for Christians to hold their faith to be true and all others to be false or at best imperfect. Many think of religion as the product of man's search for meaning in the universe in which he finds himself. Imperfect as he is, so these hold, through his search man can never fully know Reality—or, to give Reality a traditional name—God. According to this view, all religions have elements of truth, and progress is to be made by the adherents of one faith sharing with those of another what they have learned. Therefore, so the argument runs, either a new religion should be evolved, made up from all its predecessors, or Christianity should seek to incorporate the best elements of all religions.

Stern facts make this comfortable view untenable. In the first place, in their basic assumptions Christianity and the other religions are irreconcilable. For instance, a fundamental conviction of Buddhism is that life is not worth living, and that man is caught in an endless succession of births and rebirths. Salvation, accordingly, consists in breaking this succession and in bringing to an end, in Nirvana, this entity called "I." In sharp contrast, Christianity declares that life can be infinitely worth living, and that God's greatest gift to man is eternal life. In general, Hinduism, although more multiform than Christianity, is pantheistic. It holds that, taken as a whole, the universe is God, and that there is no God apart from the sum total of the universe. But Christianity, while holding that God created the world and continues to work in and through it, teaches that He is by no means identical with it. To use technical terms, Christianity believes God to be both immanent and transcendent. Confucianism, along with some other faiths, tends to be agnostic and to regard religion as man's creation: Christianity declares that the Gospel which it proclaims is God's search for man, the divine initiative.

In many ways Christianity is closest to Judaism and Islam. All three religions believe in God, in His wisdom, His righteousness, His justice, and His sovereignty in the universe which He has made. Yet, in contrast with them both, Christianity holds that in Jesus God was incarnate, that in him God inaugurated a new order, His reign, or His kingdom, and that in the incarnation, the life, the death, and the resurrection of Jesus God wrought man's redemption. Judaism cannot grant this, or it would cease to be Judaism and would become Christianity. At most it regards Jesus as one of its prophets. Mohammed said flatly that

God cannot have a son. He held that the gulf between God and man is so great that it cannot be bridged; whereas Christianity declares as its central affirmation that in Jesus God has bridged that gulf. So different are these non-Christian faiths even from one another that they cannot be combined without doing violence to the central affirmations of each. To seek to incorporate them in Christianity would be to denature both them and Christianity. Any attempt at fusing Christianity with these others means bringing them together on a basis of superficial similarities which ignores basic convictions. The result would be anemic, quite lacking in compelling conviction or in the ability to win or to hold the allegiance of men.

Many attempts at such a synthesis of Christianity with other faiths have been made, but never has any of the resulting systems possessed continuing vitality. Thus what were known as the Ebionites sought to confine the new wine of the Gospel in the old wineskins of Judaism. After a few generations they disappeared. In the early centuries many endeavored to fit Jesus into a current popular religious philosophy and in doing so gave rise to a wide variety of movements which bear the collective name of Gnostic. It may well have been that for a time the Gnostics were more numerous than those who were not willing so to accommodate the Christian faith to the contemporary religious scene. Yet all the various types of Gnosticism died out so completely that we know them chiefly from the writings of their Christian critics. So also did their contemporaries, the Marcionites. The past century saw the Brahmo Samaj, a high-minded attempt to combine Christianity with Hinduism. Although it produced a great poet and saint, Rabindranath Tagore, it has been confined to a small group of intellectuals, has had no kindling contagion, and has been a fading feature of the Indian scene.

To be sure, Christianity has been influenced by its milieu. Indeed, what we call Christianity is a combination of the Gospel with the various environments in which the Gospel has obtained followers. Thus in its intellectual formulations much of Christianity bears the impress of the philosophy of the Greco-Roman civilization in which it won its first great victories. In their organization the churches in which are still to be found the majority of Christians reflect something of the structure which the Catholic Church developed in the Roman Empire. Yet those elements or features which are derived from a particular environment ultimately prove a handicap, for as that environment passes they become anachronisms. The Gospel survives, ageless. It is true that the Gospel is closely tied to history. That is an essential feature of the Incarnation. The very fact that the Word became flesh means that the central events of the Gospel occurred at a particular time and in a particular setting. But here the environment was made to contribute to what Christians hold to be the divine purpose. Always, so Christians affirm, in the deeds which constitute the Gospel story God was master and made the milieu serve His ends. The more any church makes the Gospel central and subordinates the environment to the Gospel, the greater will be the continuing vigor of that church.

Yet always even the most vital forms of Christianity have displayed to some degree the influence of their environment. We often speak of the Orthodox churches as Greek. Certainly they carry with them much which they inherited from the Greek outlook on the universe. Similarly the Roman Catholic Church clearly perpetuates the Roman mind and temper. The Church of England has both shaped and been shaped by the English spirit.

Presumably this will continue to be so. As it becomes

firmly rooted in any particular land or people Christianity will take on something of the complexion of the cultural heritage of that area. Indeed, this is already occurring in lands where Christianity is of recent transplanting or planting. Thus the Christianity of the United States, while clearly descended from it, differs from that of Europe. In the United States the Christianity of the Negroes has distinctive features which are derived from the Negroes and the social and economic background and setting of the Negroes. Of this the Negro spirituals are a striking example. In the United States, moreover, the churches reflect the social patterns of the white stock. Each denomination appeals to particular economic and social strata. In China much of Protestantism places emphasis, as has Confucianism, upon the production of moral character and the saving of society through good men. Other phases of Chinese Protestantism appear to reflect the Buddhist concern for individual salvation for the world to come. The fact that in India Protestant Christianity has drawn the overwhelming majority of its members from the depressed classes explains much of the character of the Protestant churches of that land. In South Africa the proliferation of Protestant sects among the Bantus is in part a reflection of the traditional Bantu mind and social structure. We may expect that the world-wide Christianity of the future will continue to be varied and that it will be in part regional and, so long as nations continue, national.

Under these circumstances, will a Christianity which has drawn all mankind to professed allegiance be able to achieve world-wide unity? Will all men through it become a single brotherhood? Will there be an all-embracing Church which will know no strife of parties or nations or theologies and no rivalries among strong leaders? Obviously that time is at best very far distant. The gulf between non-Roman Catholics and Roman Catholics, to mention only one of the chief traditional divisions, persists. Here and there individuals and small groups partly transcend it through a common allegiance to Christ and association in action, as in Germany, in face of a common peril. Yet it gives no sign of disappearing. However, today is witnessing, as we have seen, the rapid growth of a series of movements through which non-Roman Catholic Christians are coming together and which here and there are reaching out to Roman Catholics and are embracing a few of them. These movements give hope of progress toward a Christian unity which is more inclusive than any which Christians have thus far known. Indeed, as through them Christians of varying ecclesiastical traditions come together, they find, almost to their surprise, that a common spirit exists of which they had not been aware and which ecclesiastical structures have obscured. A much larger unity is already in being than is generally realized. Through observing these movements we can begin to have hope that, in spite of historic divisions, a unity embracing all Christians will some time be achieved. Just how or when it will come we cannot know, but, watching as we now do the reversal of the progressive division which has heretofore characterized Christianity and the beginning of an integration of the Christian forces, we have tangible reasons for confidence, still somewhat hesitant, that a real and visible unity will be attained.

The precise organizational and institutional forms which this unity will take we cannot know. Presumably no one form or set of forms will be final. So long as the living Spirit—what Christians call the Holy Spirit—continues to operate within the Christian community, new organizations will appear and changes will be made to meet fresh conditions in the human scene. If the time ever comes when new movements do not appear and institutional patterns do not vary, it will be because Christianity has become sterile and the living Spirit has departed from it.

While we cannot know the distant forms which the organizational and institutional expression of Christian unity will take, by viewing the past we can read certain lessons. We can discern which of the proposed roads toward Christian unity will prove to be blind alleys and we can discern which of them holds hope of progress toward the desired goal.

First of all it seems clear that unity is not to be achieved through conformation to any one of the existing ecclesiastical patterns. As we have seen, the Roman Catholic Church is the most nearly inclusive of the attempts of that kind and yet an ever smaller proportion of those who profess and call themselves Christians are to be found within its borders. Where it has failed no other church is likely to succeed. The more rigid the structure and the more sweeping the claims, the less is the likelihood of all Christians conforming. Even a fairly flexible structure, if it holds to an irreducible minimum, will fare but little better.

Here we must consider the dream symbolized by the word "reunion." Many Christians, especially of the Anglican communion, in working for Christian unity have as their goal what they seek to express by that word. As they look back into history they believe they see a time when all Christians were in one visible church. That church, they hold, was Catholic or universal. Structurally it was held together by an episcopate which claimed historical continuity from the Apostles and to have the authority of Christ himself. It formulated its faith in certain great verbal affirmations, notably the Apostles' Creed and the Nicene Creed. It administered the sacraments, chief of which were baptism and the Lord's Supper. The latter depended for its validity and efficacy upon a ministry ordained by bishops in the historic succession. The faith was to be found in the Bible, the Holy Scriptures, the revealed word of God. That Catholic Church was eventually rent by division after division— by heresies which tore away segments such as the Nestorians, the Copts, and the Armenians, by the slow drifting apart of East and West, by the Protestant secession, and by the hardening of dogma in the Roman Church which gave to the Bishop of Rome an autocratic power which he had not originally possessed. Unity, therefore, so these Christians aver, is to be achieved by reuniting the severed branches of that Catholic Church. This is to be accomplished by all Christians returning to the features which gave that church its Catholic or universal character. To the support of this interpretation of history and this dream is brought vast erudition. On it many saintly souls pin their hopes and to it they direct their prayers. Its four points, outlined in what is called the Lambeth Quadrilateral, have been offered by the Bishops of the Anglican communion to the Christians of the world as the basis of "reunion." This program is not to be dismissed lightly but is to be treated with respect.

Yet this dream of "reunion" is subject to the basic weakness of the Roman Catholic way to unity. It is the attempt to bring all Christians to conformity with an existing ecclesiastical pattern. The pattern is less elaborate than that presented by the Roman Catholic Church and allows for greater variations. But it is essentially that of the Church of England and its daughter churches of the Anglican communion. It has not achieved the unity of Christians in England or in any other land where it is to be found. There appears to be no more likelihood of its winning the assent of all Christians than does the method proposed by the Roman Catholic Church. To be sure, some degree of fellowship has been obtained with several of the Eastern churches and with the Church of Sweden. Yet although the Church of South India was constituted by a fairly close approximation to the standards set by the Lambeth Quadrilateral, it is declared not to be in communion with the Church of England because it does not fully conform to them, and the breach is not healed.

This "Catholic" pattern was developed to meet a particular set of circumstances at one stage of the history of the Church. The word Catholic is put in quotation marks here to stress this fact. It means, as I have said, universal. Theoretically when applied to the Church it means the Universal Church—the community which includes all Christians. However, since no organization, not even the little company at Jerusalem up to and including the day of Pentecost, has embraced all the avowed disciples of Christ, and since those who use the term "Catholic" as a prefix to "Church" claim by it that their branch of the church is identical with the Universal Church or at least is the norm for that Church and that other ecclesiastical bodies are schisms or heresies, "Catholic" in fact acquires a partisan and therefore a sectarian flavor. What was first called the "Catholic" Church sought to safeguard the Christian Gospel against the attempts at compromise which were represented by the Gnostics and the Marcionites. In this it seemed to have success. These variants of Christianity disappeared and for a brief time the majority of Christians were to be found within its structure. Yet one of the chief early variants, Arianism, also used the word "Catholic" to designate its branch of the Church. As I have suggested, the death of the variants from the "Catholic" Church was due to their inherent weakness as combinations of transient cosmologies and cosmogenies with the Gospel which so denatured the latter that they passed with a change in the intellectual climate rather than to the particular form of organization of the Church which held more closely to the Gospel. Indeed, some and perhaps most of these variants were episcopally organized and claimed apostolic succession for their bishops. Moreover, as we have also seen, the "Catholic" structure owed much of its cohesion and inclusiveness to the circumstance that it was within a political framework which antedated it, the Roman Empire. Even then it never embraced all who called themselves Christians. "Reunion" of this "Catholic" Church, if that impossibility could be accomplished by turning back the wheels of history, would leave outside it many authentically Christian saints.

Before the Roman Empire broke up, the "Catholic" Church began to disintegrate. In its attempt to safeguard the Gospel it expelled a substantial minority, the Arians, and such smaller and yet impressive minorities as the Nestorians and Monophysites. Many among these dissident churches undoubtedly bore the fruits of the spirit—love, joy, peace, long-suffering, gentleness, faithfulness, meekness, and self-control—which are conclusive evidence that they were really Christians. We need only to recall the great missionary to the Goths, Ulfilas, an Arian.

When the Roman Empire dwindled and disintegrated the Catholic Church also broke into fragments. To be sure, it did not become quite as divided as did the political structure. Its western wing, the Roman Catholic Church, embraced almost all of western Europe at a time when the region was characterized by scores of political entities, large and small. Its eastern wing spread outside the narrow confines of the Byzantine Empire, a political heir of the Roman Empire, and held in an imperfect yet real unity the family of Orthodox churches. Yet neither the western nor the eastern wing of the "Catholic" Church succeeded in retaining in its fellowship all Christians in its area. This was especially true of the western wing. Not only did it not hold the Protestants, but also, even during the Middle Ages, it expelled some of the choicest Christian spirits. The hope of a "reunion" of the severed branches of a "Catholic" Church through a method which has proved so great a failure in the past seems foredoomed by its history.

Then, too, the nineteenth- and twentieth-century course of Christianity more and more precludes the possibility of the success of the effort to bring all Christians together through this "Catholic" pattern. The most rapid expansion of Christianity in the past hundred and fifty years has been through churches which have repudiated the historic episcopate and apostolic succession. The greatest numerical growth and much of the vigor of Christianity in that period has been in the United States. Here, even when the Roman Catholic Church is included, the churches which hold to apostolic succession and the historic episcopate are in the minority. If only non-Roman Catholics are counted, they are in the very small minority. The overwhelming majority of non-Roman Catholic Christians in the United States are in such fellowships as those of the Baptists, the Methodists, the Disciples of Christ, the Congregational-Christian churches, various churches of the Reformed and Presbyterian tradition, and the Lutherans. None of the great American Lutheran bodies have bishops, and the Methodists, who call their general superintendents bishops, make no claim that the latter are in the historic succession of the "Catholic" Church. To most of the other bodies the very word "bishop" is anathema. Many of these bodies hold to the Apostles' Creed, but when in using that creed they repeat the word "Catholic" they think of it as meaning "universal" and in no sense as identical with what strict Anglicans, Orthodox, and Roman Catholics intend by it. Recent and current experience in the Church of South India, in Ceylon, and in negotiations between the Presbyterian Church in the

United States of America and the Protestant Episcopal Church in the United States might seem to hold out hope that some Baptists, Presbyterians, Methodists, and Congregationalists will be willing to fit into a much modified pattern of the Anglican interpretation of the "Catholic" tradition. Yet there seems not the slightest prospect that the majority of the Protestants of the United States will do so.

Moreover, the greatest spread of non-Roman Catholic Christianity in non-Occidental lands has been by Protestants who do not assent to the historic episcopate and apostolic succession. In China, Japan, the Philippines, Latin America, Indonesia, and much of Africa those who hold to the historic episcopate are in the small minority among non-Roman Catholic Christians. In the International Missionary Council, the most representative association of non-Occidental churches and their parent "older" churches of the Occident, those conforming to the historic episcopate are also very much in the minority.

In other words, it must be said that "reunion" as the achievement of a Christian unity which is regarded as once existing, but since lost, is contrary to historic actualities. As a means, through the historic episcopate and apostolic succession, of bringing all Christians, even all non-Roman Christians, into one visible structure, it is contrary to history and present fact.

In making this seemingly dogmatic assertion, the author must repeat that he is not unaware of the prodigious scholarship which has been brought to the defense of the "Catholic" conviction. That conviction and the evidence adduced in its support are not to be brushed aside with a sweep of the hand. We must remember that thousands of learned and devout souls have believed and continue to believe that the faith as it has been held in the "Catholic" tradition is the true Christian faith and that any departure from it is a departure from the Gospel. These same souls find that faith defined in the historic creeds and nourish their spiritual life upon the sacraments, and especially upon the Eucharist, as the divinely appointed means of grace. Many of them regard the apostolic succession of the episcopate as of the very essence of the Church of Christ. Others would not regard it to be demonstrably of Christ's explicit appointment, but hold that the utility of the historic episcopate has been so proved by the experience of the centuries that to dispense with it is to imperil the life of the Church.

This scholarship and these convictions are not being fully dealt with here not because they are unimportant but partly because they cannot be adequately summarized and examined point by point in a book of necessarily limited dimensions and partly because repeatedly through the centuries they have been argued against by scholarly and authentically Christian spirits. Full agreement is not to be reached in that fashion. We can advance toward Christian unity not by again engaging in these well-worn controversies but by coming at them from the fresh view of the progress made toward Christian unity in the past century and a half, from the challenge and the situation of our day, and from the light which the experience of the Christian community seems to shed on the future. In that, we believe, we are simply pointing out what is there to be discerned by all who make themselves familiar with the facts.

This in no sense means that those in the "Catholic" tradition do not have much to contribute to the emerging World Christian community. They do. Their sense of continuity in the Christian faith, the deposit of experience in creeds and other more elaborate theological formulations in defining the Gospel, the rich experience embodied in the historic liturgies, the records of lives who have displayed the fruit of the Spirit, the loyalty to the Incarnation and to the redemption wrought in Christ, and the wealth and depth of the Holy Communion, for these the world-wide Christian community is infinitely the richer and without them it would be immeasurably the poorer.

If Christian unity is not to be achieved by conformity with the Anglican interpretation of the "Catholic" tradition, neither is it to be attained by the adoption of any other of the existing ecclesiastical patterns. More than once we have pointed out that it is clearly fantastic to hope that Christian unity will come by conformity with the Roman Catholic Church. Some Roman Catholics hold that all professedly Christian bodies which dissent from their church will perish. That, they declare, has already been the fate of many dissidents and eventually the others will follow them in the road to dusty death. They hold that the Roman Catholic Church, sure of Christ's commission, can afford to be patient, and that to her a few centuries more or less are unimportant. Yet, as we have seen, across the centuries a progressively smaller proportion of Christians are to be found within the Roman Catholic Church, and the terrific blows dealt in the present century to southwestern Europe, the center of its traditional strength, may indicate that even this form of Christianity is transitory. Still more fantastic would be the hope that all Christians will take one of the Orthodox or other Eastern churches for their pattern, or accept, even in a modified form, any of the Protestant embodiments of the faith.

Not only the Anglican but also the other representatives of the "Catholic" tradition have a great deal to offer the world-wide Christian community. So, too, most of the forms of Protestantism can make positive contributions from their experience, their special emphases, and their saints. Much of modern Protestantism bears witness in its hymnals,

its literature on the Bible, its theology, and its devotional
life to its ability and eagerness to learn from great minds
and spirits of many different ecclesiastical traditions. Especially do such bodies as the World's Student Christian
Federation, the International Missionary Council, and the
World Council of Churches draw widely from many
branches of the Church. Here is the true catholicity, an
alertness to "what the Spirit saith to the churches," which
may well be a foretaste of the fashion in which the world
Christian community will take advantage of what Christians of all lands and ages and ecclesiastical heritages have
learned and thought and done.

It does not seem probable that the next step toward unity
is what is often called "organic union," the fusion of existing ecclesiastical structures into one. To be sure, the present
century has seen an increasing number of such fusions. The
United Church of Canada, the Church of South India, the
Church of Christ in China, and the Church of Christ in
Japan are notable examples. Each of these has combined
bodies of widely differing ecclesiastical traditions. Yet none
has drawn together all Christians or even all Protestant
Christians in its country or area, nor does it seem about
to do so. The procedure results in new ecclesiastical structures of fairly traditional patterns, and, as we have seen,
this road toward Christian unity has repeatedly proved a
blind alley.

Again and again the hope has been expressed that unity
would come if Christians were to return to New Testament
Christianity. If by New Testament Christianity is meant
the ideal held up for the Church as the perfect expression
of the spirit of Christ, we could gladly agree. It is pre-
cisely as the Church becomes the perfect continuation of the
Incarnation, the full embodiment of Christ and of his self-
giving, redeeming love that it becomes a visible expression

of Christian unity. But if by New Testament Christianity is meant, as is usually the case, the reproduction of the early church as we see it pictured in the New Testament, then that road also ends in frustration. This is partly because the church of which we catch glimpses in the New Testament was neither united nor uniform. It had not achieved Christian unity. Its divisions and dissensions are all too painfully evident. It is also partly because no one type of ecclesiastical organization is uniform in the churches described in the New Testament. Then, too, the variety of ecclesiastical bodies which claim New Testament precedent and authority proves that Christians will not agree on what visible forms reproduce New Testament Christianity.

How, then, is Christian unity to be attained? If it is not to come through the conformation by all Christians to any existing ecclesiastical tradition, by conscious fusions of existing churches into new ecclesiastical bodies, or by a return to the patterns of organization and worship of the Christianity of the first century as discerned in the pages of the New Testament, by what means is it to be achieved? Obviously it will have tangible expressions. Clearly, too, these tangible expressions will include intellectual formulations of the faith, patterns of worship, and a visible structure. What are these to be? We cannot know certainly.

If history is still young, if the human race has untold thousands of years before it, and if Christianity is to continue to spread and ultimately to prevail, any forecast of the details of what forms the world-wide Church is to take is almost certainly to be disproved by the event. On the other hand, if history is nearly spent, if man's course on this planet is nearly done, or if Christianity is to disappear, then we are not to see on this earth the fulfillment of the dream embodied in the Great Commission: a mankind-embracing Christian unity, now so hopefully incipient, will not be realized, and any attempt to speculate on its visible aspects will be made in the face of certain frustration.

If one believes that the weight of evidence favors the hopeful view of the future of human beings and the Christian community, the manifest inability to foretell the far distant forms which Christianity is to take need not discourage us from seeking to discern the direction which the movement toward Christian unity is taking. If we can perceive this direction we can act more wisely. Certain generalizations which will help us to ascertain this direction appear to arise from the history which we have been summarizing and the analyses which we have been venturing.

First of all, Christian unity seems to be coming about through a variety of ways. To date no one organization has proved comprehensive. The nearest approach to inclusiveness of all varieties of Christians is the World Council of Churches and that by no means embraces all Christians. The Roman Catholic Church, some of the strongest Protestant churches, and several of the Orthodox churches including the largest of all, that of Russia, are among those bodies which are still not within it. Yet in many ways Christians are coming together, locally, regionally, nationally, and globally. Some organizations are ones in which Christians work together as individuals, not officially representing the churches. Of these the Young Men's and Young Women's Christian Associations and various student Christian movements, including the comprehensive World's Student Christian Federation, are examples. In others the churches are officially represented, either directly or indirectly. Of these such national bodies as the Federal Council of the Churches of Christ in America, the British Council of Churches, and the National Christian Council of India are outstanding instances. On the world scale the International Missionary Council and the World Council of

Churches are the most nearly comprehensive. Still other movements for Christian unity are the actual merging of existing ecclesiastical bodies into a new body. Most of these are unions of churches of the same ecclesiastical family, such as those of Methodists in Great Britain and the United States. Others are fusions of bodies of dissimilar traditions. Of these the Church of South India and the Church of Christ in Japan are the most nearly comprehensive. In these many ways Christians are being brought together as never before in study, in worship, and in action. They are learning to understand and to trust one another. They are discovering a deeper and wider community of faith than they believed existed.

In the next place, most of these ways of achieving unity are relatively recent. They do not antedate the eighteenth century and most of them are the creation of the twentieth century. Here is a movement which is gaining momentum. Christianity is proving that it is both flexible and vital. So vigorous and so novel is the movement that Christians may well believe that the Holy Spirit, seeing the failure of the old methods of achieving the unity which should characterize the Christian community, is opening fresh channels and in the day of mankind's desperate need is creating new agencies to spread the Gospel, to make it effective in the life of mankind, and to bring into being a world-embracing fellowship of faith, hope, and love.

The sweep toward Christian unity springs, as we have seen, from Protestantism, which is at once the most divided and the most flexible wing of the Church. It is also the most rapidly growing branch of Christianity. In this flexibility is an indication that the movement will not be choked by loyalty to stereotyped ecclesiastical forces and in this growth is a prophecy that unity will also increase.

In the movement toward Christian unity the main

branches of the Christian Church are preserving their identity and are continuing their witness to the special emphases
which have been theirs. The chief families of Protestantism
(Lutheran, Reformed and Presbyterian, Anglican, Methodist, Baptist, Congregationalist, to mention only the most
prominent), most of the numerically minor kinds of Protestantism, the various Eastern churches, including the
Orthodox, and the Old Catholic bodies retain their identity.

This differs from the movement of the first centuries
which issued in the Catholic Church of the Roman Empire.
That was not so much an effort to achieve unity as it was an
attempt to define the Christian faith and to assure adherence to it by all who called themselves Christians. Variants from the "Catholic" faith were denounced as in error
and were expected to die out.

In the early days of the faith such a procedure had features to commend it but it is no longer either imperative or
advisable. In the first centuries, Christianity was comparatively unformed in its worship, in the intellectual formulations of its faith, and in its organization. It was thus that
it had come into the world, for it had entered history not
as a system of thought or as an organization but as a Life
and as a community centering about that Life. Until Christians had thought through the significance of that Life,
there was danger that the essence of the Gospel might be
lost or seriously compromised. This was the peril of Gnosticism and, a little later, of Arianism. Thanks to the discussions of these early centuries, those books which we call the
New Testament were discerned as the authentic records of
the Gospel and handed down to the Church for all time.
Through these discussions, too, the issues were clearly defined and statements, or creeds, were formulated and accepted by the majority of Christians as in accord with the
Gospel on the points at issue. These creeds have become a

continuing feature of the Christian heritage. In its day the organization through which the New Testament was transmitted and the creeds supported were important. As we have seen, however, they did not preserve Christian unity.

Now that the New Testament is firmly established in the life and faith of the Christian community and now that the great creeds and liturgies have become integral in the structure of so many communions, what is needed is not so much a structure which will safeguard them as one which will further the unity of all Christians. In that structure room must be found for the contributions of all the varied historic expressions of the Christian faith. It must as well be sufficiently flexible not only to preserve the heritage of the past but also to allow for fresh movements of the Spirit in the future.

In a certain rough parallel the religious scene in the United States epitomizes the world-wide trends in the Christianity of our day. Here almost all the existing forms of Christianity are represented. Here they rub shoulder to shoulder on a basis of legal equality: none receives special assistance from the state as against the others. This close juxtaposition and this legal equality are the direction in which the current is setting the world around. Here, as in the world at large, close proximity works on the one hand for the interpenetration of one form of Christianity by another and for cooperation, and on the other makes for heightened antagonism and the hardening of the resistance to cooperation. The opposition to cooperation is seen in certain wings of Protestantism, notably several of the Lutheran and Baptist bodies, Fundamentalist circles, and Anglo-Catholics. It is also seen in the Eastern churches and particularly in the Roman Catholic Church. In the United States, too, Roman Catholics, while prominent and aggressive, are proportionately not growing as rapidly as are Protestants. So it is in the world taken as a whole. In Protestantism the increase is most marked in what might be called the extreme wing of that branch of the Christian faith rather than through its classical expressions—Lutheranism, Anglicanism, and the Reformed and Presbyterian bodies. This, too, is true in the global scene. Moreover, the United States is a microcosm of the world-wide Church in the fashion in which fellowship is mounting, both informally and through organizations, by outright mergers of existing denominations, and by increasing cooperation among ecclesiastical bodies.

In the very novelty of the ways through which Christians are coming together is a ground for hope that world-wide Christian unity will be progressively achieved. The fact that the movement is transcending existing divisions, crystallized as they are in history and in ancient controversies, is a basis for confidence. Increasingly Christians of many different ecclesiastical bodies are joining in the Communion: the Lord's table, long a symbol of division, is becoming a symbol and means of a larger unity. The movement does not come out of indifference to the tenets of the various churches: it has sprung not from the rank and file of the laity, who might be supposed to hold lightly the historic differences, but from the leaders, those who presumably have the greatest stake in the perpetuation of the divisions. Nor is it born of the fear that if a common front is not presented the enemies of the faith will triumph: rather has it arisen from the purpose of giving the Gospel to the entire world and the glad confidence that the Gospel is for all men.

We cannot know what visible forms the movement for Christian unity will ultimately take. We can be reasonably sure that all of its present expressions must be regarded as transitional. If such an ecclesiastical structure as the Roman Catholic Church, at one stage useful, has now become an obstacle to Christian unity, the same will be true of any organization if it is regarded as the final word, the one instrument through which God would work for the achievement of love among Christians. Organizations must change to meet the shifting demands of varying environments. If they do not change they will be left behind. They may endure but if so it will be as fossils, sterile survivals of a bygone age, speaking less and less to their times. Christianity is a living faith. As such it must continue to give rise to new forms to meet the shifting conditions of successive fresh environments. As we have reminded ourselves, Christianity is a religion compounded of the Gospel, which is eternal and does not change, and of adjustments to a particular culture and age. The persistence and growth of Christianity depend on the one hand on loyalty to the Gospel and on the other hand on the ability to adapt forms and methods to the demands of particular areas and eras. One of the many grounds for optimism in the present movement for Christian unity is the flexibility of the organizations through which it is being expressed. New structures are continually emerging for bringing Christians together. Fresh combinations of structures, themselves of recent origin, are being made. Thus in the United States a number of nation-wide cooperative undertakings are in process of being brought together into a larger whole. So it will be as long as Christianity is vigorous, to the very end of time. No one set of patterns will give final and perfect expression to the urge for world-wide Christian fellowship. The life inherent in the Christian community will from time to time move in new ways to further the love which is of the essence of the Christian faith.

This is as it should be. It is of the nature of the Gospel that it can never be identified with any one organization.

Organization can facilitate fellowship and true Christian unity, but it cannot of itself achieve that unity. Some of the greatest denials of the unity which is love are to be found within ecclesiastical structures. For example, as we have seen, behind the façade of unity presented by the great Roman Catholic Church are jealousies, strife, and bitterness between orders, between individuals, and between national groups. If true Christian unity is that of love the Roman Catholic Church is by no means a perfect example of unity. The same is, unfortunately, true of all other ecclesiastical bodies. Even the Society of Friends, which seems at the opposite extreme from the Roman Catholic Church in its tolerance and its lack of emphasis on organization and which in our day has given so notable an example of self-forgetting, loving service to sufferers from war, has its inner dissensions. Organization may and often does help the achievement of Christian unity. Yet organizations may be and often are obstacles to Christian unity. The emphasis must always be not on organization but on the love which is distinctive of the Gospel, the love which is humble, grateful, wondering response to the love of God in Christ. As Christians dwell on God's forgiving and redeeming love they are impelled to show love to all men and "especially toward those who are of the household of faith," for "he who loveth not his brother whom he hath seen, how can he love God whom he hath not seen?"

Is God's will to prevail? It is God's purpose, so Christians must believe, to bring into being a community of love, the love which is in response to God's love expressed in the Incarnation, the crucifixion, and the resurrection. God wishes that community to display the fruits of the Spirit— love, joy, peace, long-suffering, kindness, goodness, faithfulness, meekness, self-control. He desires that it should be without spot or blemish. Is the will of God to be perfectly accomplished in the Church? To those who know the churches of history and of our own day this dream seems so far from being realized as to appear beyond the possible. Yet Christian faith must believe that God cannot be defeated. His purposes may be delayed but they will be attained. It may be that history will be brought to an end before the community of perfect love embracing all mankind will be realized. But if not within history, then beyond it in that reach of existence into which we can penetrate only by faith, God's will is to be done and the community of adoration, thanksgiving, and love is fully to reflect the self-giving love of God. Even now that community is here, still imperfect and divided, but in part a foretaste of what is to be. Daily men and women are entering it through the new birth. To those who have eyes to see, it is present and growing. Usually it is not noticed by those who write our newspapers or who command the time of our radios. Yet it is a reality. It and its progress are the true meaning of the human drama and the hope of our bewildered and distraught race.

# INDEX